VANISHING
GREECE

VANISHING
GREECE

PHOTOGRAPHS BY
CLAY PERRY

INTRODUCTION BY
PATRICK LEIGH FERMOR

TEXT BY
ELIZABETH BOLEMAN-HERRING

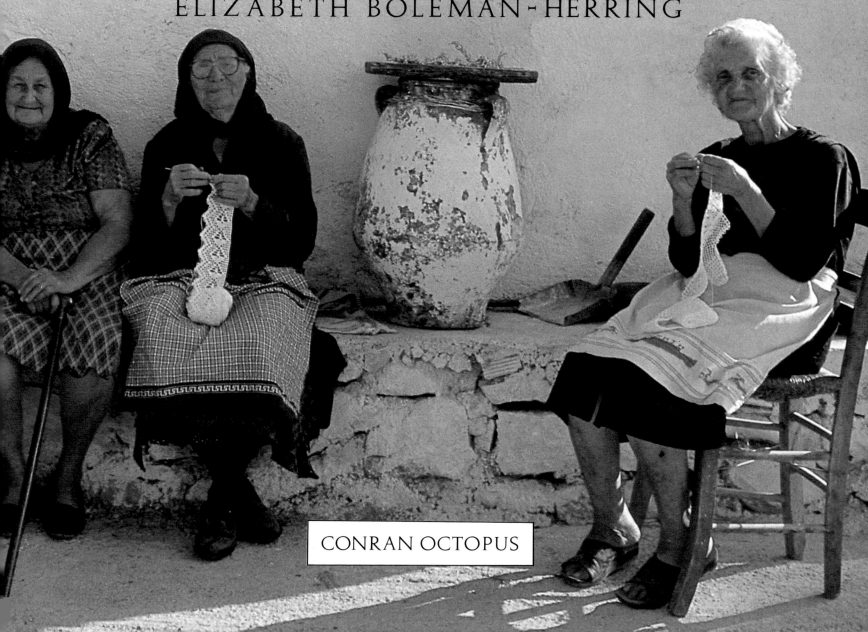

CONRAN OCTOPUS

TO MAGGIE
I would like to dedicate this book to my wife Maggie who has been a constant companion on my Greek journeys. Without her help and support this book would not have been possible.

First published in 1991 by
Conran Octopus Limited
37 Shelton Street
London WC2H 9HN

PROJECT EDITOR **JOANNA BRADSHAW**
EDITORIAL ASSISTANT **ROD MACKENZIE**
ART EDITOR **KAREN BOWEN**
MAP ILLUSTRATOR **PAUL BRYANT**
PRODUCTION **JULIA GOLDING**

British Library Cataloguing in Publication Data
Perry, Clay
    Vanishing Greece.
    1. Greece. Social conditions
    I. Title   II. Boleman-Herring, Elizabeth
949.076

ISBN 1-85029-336-8

Printed and bound in Singapore
Typeset by Hunters Armley Limited
Colour separation by Chroma Graphics
(Overseas) Pty Ltd

CONTENTS

FOREWORD

ONE DAY, HIGH ON MOUNT OLYMPOS, ZEUS HEARD OF THE wickedness and greed of men, and decided that if it was true, he would destroy mankind, as the gods despise greed and selfishness. Zeus took his son Hermes, the messenger, and together they descended into the world of mortals disguised as poor wayfarers. They were scorned and abused by the rich who lived in the cities and Zeus became convinced that mankind must indeed be destroyed. They came to a humble cottage which was inhabited by an old peasant couple named Baucis and Philemon, who invited the strangers in and gave them the last of their food and wine. After they had eaten and drank, Hermes miraculously renewed the wine in the pitcher. So it was that Baucis and Philemon realized that they were in the presence of gods, rather than poor mortal travellers. Because of their generosity, Zeus decided not to destroy the world of men, and the old couple were made priest and priestess of the Temple of Zeus, into which he transformed their humble home. Some say that when Baucis and Philemon became very old the god turned them into trees, others that they were transformed into stars in the heavens, but the legend lives on in Greece, as does the hospitality (*philoxenia*).

I have met Baucis and Philemon many times on my journeys through Greece, sharing their last dry *paximadi* (rusks), a little goats' milk, some cheese and a few olives. In a way they are the essence of rural Greece, and have changed little since the time of the ancients. Sadly though, the time-honoured landscape that would have been as familiar to Homer as to Katzanzakis *is* changing. The windmills stand idle or crumble into decay; the threshing floor is lost beneath the undergrowth and modern concrete villas are filling the landscape. Greek pragmatism and love of the new is changing the Hellenic world more quickly than ever before. Within a generation the donkey has become a rarity in many places, and the quiet fishing village is now a hustle of tourist shops and cafés. Something essential is changing. It is these changes, observed over 18 years, that have urged me to record as much as I could of this vanishing world.

This book is not intended to be a guide or a travelogue, although I have included some familiar images that are quintessentially Greek. It is more of a personal odyssey, and my search for archaic images has been dictated by the fates, pulling me more to one place than to another, sometimes to be disappointed, sometimes to be richly rewarded. Because of this, there are some areas of Greece which I have barely touched upon, and others that are well represented, but I hope that the photographs will give the reader at least a glimpse of a very special place that really is our common European home.

CLAY PERRY
LONDON, APRIL 1991

INTRODUCTION

MANY YEARS AGO, LIVING IN THE HOUSE OF THE PAINTER NIKO Ghika, on the island of Hydra, I was constantly comparing the sea, the buildings, the rocks and the trees all around me with their representation in the pictures that hung on the walls or filled page after page of the heavy art books on the shelves. I wondered how he had managed to convey all these things with such brilliant success, and tried to sort out my thoughts on paper. I began as follows: 'Mediterranean lands are a most paintable region. The vapours that roam the Italian air deepen the colours of the landscape, soften and liquify the outline of things and temper the antagonism of light and shade. This density establishes a limit to the sky and invests the country with a soft and elegiac lyricism that makes it most pictorially amenable. Under this heavier sky, cypresses fall into line, castles rise on their cones, towers ascend, and machicolations spread; looping through a georgic champaign, the bridge-spanned rivers uncoil; domes rise into the umbered evening, dusk spins its cobwebs in the valleys. Inert and beautiful, the landscape has been softened up for the assault.

'Greece,' I went on, 'is the opposite. It is a source of confusion that the two peninsulas, so similar in geology and flora, should be so unlike. Greece is wilder and harder, less vegetated, more precipitous. Plains are scarcer, mountain ranges soar from the sea into bare wildernesses and the dark khaki *macchia* which dulls the contours of Italian mountains and turns them the colour of camouflaged army trucks, is largely absent. The anatomy of ranges juts into the air as bare and hard as bones. But the difference lies elsewhere.

'It lies in the light. Low and bright, the large sun spins in a sky of pale and unfathomable blue drained of all but radiance. It mounts to infinity and showers down a volley of universal and crystalline light that strips and hardens the unblunted commotions of mineral and chisels them into innumerable facets; then, penetrating their armour, it makes them transparent, and, in spite of their interweaving of hard salients, as light on the water from which they spring – which too, is splintered and immaterialized by the onslaught of the sky – as smoke. The air enclosing these mountains is alive and electrifying. A stranger feels himself surrounded by crackling volatility which ascends to outer space. These ecstatic properties, which are hard to apprehend or examine by reason, put the country beyond all danger of confusion with Tuscany, Calabria, Andalusia or Provence and make it, for those who know it well, the most beautiful of countries. It is also this phenomenon which, rightly, after a sequence of failures, daunts a painter and makes Greece one of the world's most unpaintable territories.

'How, then,' I went on, 'should this particular siege be conducted? How can those staring and wonderful skies be captured, those flaring and miraculous seas? A frontal attack lands the painter with results that are akin to the scorching scenery, the stage properties and the rhetoric of the many tons of northbound picture-postcards which, every summer, clog the post offices of the Mediterranean Sea.' Success, it struck me, could only be achieved by stratagems, by penetration in detail, by sapping and enfilading, by ambush and escalade and by secret intelligence with the beleaguered. Avoiding, as his main target, the single phenomenon of the light and concentrating on its incidental relationship with matter, Ghika had captured it almost casually, as a corollary of his central purpose.

The wonderful photographs of Clay Perry seem to me, *mutatis mutandis* and allowing for the difference that separates canvas, camel-hair and pigment from celluloid and polished glass, to have adopted something similar to these wise and devious tactics. His photographs are prompted neither by 'the Sudden View', nor by beginner's luck. He knows the ground well, he has studied all the hazards, he has lived here and put down roots; there is 'intelligence with the beleaguered', indeed, and he has discovered secrets for the control of colour and texture and light and the art of outwitting or side-stepping the pitfalls of the eternal summer which post-Byron tourists (perhaps without having read a word) all pine for. His pictures present a Greece of infinite variety, subtlety and depth. Nobody can capture the noonday devil of August with greater skill; but, by often seeking his quarry at other seasons; at dawn or dusk, or even after dark; when the skies are troubled by a storm blowing up; when the leaves are all about to be blown away; or when the earliest grass fledges the limestone, he leads us into a private Greece the tourist never sees. These pictures seem to me to be unsurpassed. As the title warns us, there is a strong hint of sadness in this wonderful sequence. They are a last, long look at Greece before many of the things that attach one to the country are swept away. Every spring, as a signal of the season, the bulldozer and the cement-mixer move into gear as the storks and the swallows and the house martins start building, and every autumn there are fewer eaves and roof-tiles left for next year's return.

For me these pages are the recapitulation of a Greek lifetime which began fifty-six years ago on my twentieth birthday, on Mount Athos, when I trudged for a month through deep snow from monastery to monastery. How well Clay Perry captures this steep peninsula, barnacled with abbeys! Their fortifications loom from the forest, whitewashed oriels project on wooden struts, cypress and orange trees crowd the wells of courtyards, and, inside, the walls under the cupolas swarm with painted saints; halos overlap like fish-scales, nimbus on nimbus, and the monks assembling at the tapping of the *semantron* beam from their tempests of beard like ancient river-gods.

This was my beginning, but, starting on the eastern shore, it jumps the gun. The book begins in the west, with sunbursts and cloudy skies over the timbered Epirote ranges near the Albanian border: Gamila, Papingo, Grammos and the Pindus watershed, the haunt of bears and deer and wolves and wild boar. Eagles hang in mid-cleft scarcely moving a feather, hermitages crowd the rock-faults like toadstools, the Aoōs and the Voidomati rivers uncoil their canyons, and sheep- and goat-bells are seldom out of ear-shot; but the wicker huts of the herdsmen, like congeries of beehives in every sheltered dip, vanished a generation ago. The nomadic life of the Sarakatsans is ending and the black-and-white geometric and prehistoric patterns of their squaws' clothing have migrated to folklore museums. Vanishing Greece indeed! Byzantine and Turkish bridges span ravines as weightlessly as rainbows, or the tracks of bouncing balls; steep paths zigzag through the beech woods to the Zagorochoria, where the honey-coloured Cotswold houses are tiled with slabs of giant slate, and bleating fills the air, horns twirl and flocks jam the lanes.

Except for impalements and pyramids of severed heads, lake-island Yanina has not changed much since Ali Pasha's day; the vistas of tall reeds, raucous with Aristophanean croaking, are the same as when the Vizir lolled in his canoe, his chibūk buried in his beard, now and then letting off his fowling piece over the oarsmens' heads while the beaters sent up a confetti of waterfowl. Hobhouse, after a rainy mountain journey, complained to Byron that nobody in the town knew how to mend an Englishman's umbrella.

Who are these elders in black homespun outside the café in Metsovo? Only one, resembling a colonel in the Brigade of Guards, is still in his flared goatshair tunic, his kalpak, kilt, white tights and tufted brogues, but they all grasp herdmens' crooks with snake tops and all their features have been scooped and scorched by the rigours of pastoral life. They are Koutzovlachs – semi-nomads, unlike the Sarakatsans, who used to have no homes but their wigwams – hobnobbing in their low-latin dialect that some say is an overflow from Romania, while others maintain the opposite; yet others uphold that the order calling the Legions of Honorius in AD 410 never reached these outposts in the Pindus; scholars are at odds.

The Meteora, those famous religious caskets lifted on twirling conglomerate pillars, mark the eastern frontier of the Pindus, which is the backbone of northern Greece; and beyond it the Thessalian plain shoots away to Olympus with scarcely an intervening molehill. Taking wing across Roumeli, Clay Perry turns in mid-air to alight on the seaward buttresses of Pelion, deep in the chestnut forests which were once the mythological home of the centaurs. The flanks of the mountains are marked by a string of woodland villages of great beauty, tall churches rise from paved and shady piazzas, and three sides of all the jutting upper storeys are casements opening on spatulate leaves and the foam of the Sporades; and there the old merchant-adventurers of Portariá and Makrinítza and Zangarádes loll in the angles of the divans that run all round, sipping their thimbles of coffee, toying with their amber beads and talking of old travels across deserts and down the Red Sea and up the Nile.

Now and then, as though to remind us of more frequented itineraries, the turn of a page reveals the Propylaea, or the Parthenon or the temple of Athene Pronoia at Delphi, or the great Mycenaean walls that converge on Agamemnon's tomb: halfway halts on the way back to wilder regions, for the towers of the Mani, where these lines are being written, are all about us: clumps of broken parallelograms, half San Giminiano and half a prehistoric

Brooklyn, springing out of a planetary land as pocked as pumice, and choked with prickly pear; a land of lizards and tortoises and scarce water and circular threshing floors and dirges, too strange and solemn and beautiful a place to be ruined. (The least said the better, lest bulldozers and mixers move in and finish the job.) Across the gulf, the Messenian peninsula tapers towards Methoni, where Frankish, Venetian and Turkish battlements enclose the cape with a battered and overgrown maze of curtain-wall, ravelin, moat and counterscarp – 'the architecture of hatred', a Greek poet has called it – ending in two machicolated octagons of different girth slotting into each other above the waves. How can Monemvasia – the Crusaders' Malmsey, sticking out from the eastern Morea under a rock which is a bastion loaded with magnificent Byzantine wreckage – so ingeniously combine historical significance, claustrophobia, and magic? A massive cincture, breached on one side by a single sally-port, drops on the other into countless transparent fathoms. A leap north-west to the Ionian Sea reveals deserted shores of such untouched beauty – enclosed by beetling cliffs, a landfall for Odysseus, known only to sea-birds and fisherman – that its name and whereabouts must stay inviolate. Turning the page, and changing archipelagos, here are the *sgraffito* Chian façades of Pyrgi, then the Cyclades are underfoot and the wide slabs of schist, outlined in whitewash, turn the winding lanes into giraffes' necks. Donkeys are loaded with flowers for girls to twist into the wreaths that deck every Greek lintel on May Day; just indoors the whitewashed vaults are blackened by the cross smoked there by candles lit at the Easter flame, which cupped hands have carried flickering home after midnight.

Symmetrical batteries of painted china and hammered brass entirely hide the parlour walls of Skyros, only a few miles from Rupert Brooke's grave, and the gestures across *kapheneion*-tables of a fisherman, in baggy oriental trousers and pillbox and sash and shod with thongs and rawhide, indicate the size of some huge but evasive catch to an audience of identically-clad but sceptical fellow-Sinbads.

Such is the variety and richness of these pictures, every one of them filled with implications and temptations to expand, that all a writer can do, as it were, is to cruise about the air and make random Icarus dives among the archipelagos, dropping into inlets where the houses pile up on either shore as two-dimensionally as they do in frescos and card-houses – white, buff, fawn, grey or russet or that singing blue they call *loulaki;* into white churches, like Our Lady of Tinos, with her jungle of gilt filigree, shiny lecterns and carved wooden rood-screens, where scores of perforating and scooping penknives loop fronds and tendrils and swags, and unloose carved thurifers and winged dominions and thrones among hares and dragons, and cranes with captured serpents twisting in their bills. Festoons of beaten-silver ex-votos mark ailments and celebrate cures – a girl in a party-frock with a crutch, bandaged boys in Sunday best, ailing babies, battered fore-arms, floating kidneys, burning hearts and broken legs, all of them put right on the feast day. A different swoop lands one in Santorin.

The page showing a bride and her bridesmaids in Karpathos – frilled and goffered and coiffed with Ravenna pendants, aproned in magenta, adorned with stomachers of fifty gold plaques and booted like Poles or Russians or Tibetans against a background of wrought wood, tiers of painted chinaware and shelves of textile dowries and bolts of cloth – suggests Bhutan or some Himalayan kingdom above the clouds; only the boy with his belled bow sawing across his three-stringed rebeck tells us that we are looking at a lyra-player from Pontus, Crete, the Cyclades or the Dodecanese…. Then the scene shifts to a remote island hillside where the dry-stone walls that separate each step of terrace ascend in a lopsided flight to a chapel where the Mass, sung once a year on the day of the saint, has assembled the priest with his swinging censer and rough acolyte and a few dozen villagers round an icon of St George, embedded in nosegays; the shew-bread is cut, each crone holds a slice. Clay Perry is particularly perceptive and deft at capturing different textures – the features of just such crones – bony physiognomies stitched together out of concentric wrinkles, scooped and socketed, tortured or genial, peering from mourning weeds or rustic finery. Or, if nobody is there – the scene at the ancient Cretan Lato is empty – the inanimate world seems alive: the great ashlars, dry-stone walls collapsing and resurrecting in a chaos of tumbled Minoan masonry, the limestone and the stonecrop and the trefoil, the green-bladed sea squill and the wild fennel, ilex and wild pear and young almond bursting out while the Cretan sierras leapfrog away under a draughty sky. Nothing could be more different than Crete and the Ionian islands, but they share a legacy of Venetian overlordship, broken off in Crete by the invading Turks: fine lintels and doorways and mouldings and huge fragments of fortification abound, and sometimes more than fragments, like the great boathouses for the Doge's galleys at Chania: tremendous vaults near the sea where the great vessels were hauled out of the water for careening and caulking; the echoing concavities are still cumbered with nautical gear, tangled russet acres of net, strings of cork floats, pitch, tar and oakum and a cat or two skulking offstage with a fish's backbone….

Clay Perry's itinerary, and mine, comes to an end with Crete and the Cretans. How unmistakable they are! Breeched and tall-booted, black-clad and head-kerchiefed, they fall naturally into postures of graceful swagger; yet, settled round a table on rush-bottomed chairs, this vainglory is belied by the benevolence of their glance, and a captivating mixture of alacrity, wisdom and the comic sense. Here they are, on Ida or the White Mountains, in rough stone cheese-huts that resemble small Sardinian nuraghs or sawn-off Apulian trulli. Their fires blaze in the dark, the assembled brass bells of each herd strike a different chord, and each herdsman can tell his own flock from leagues away. Brass alembics twist above the kindled sticks, the distilled raki is piped into vast Minoan amphorae, and a great-grandmother with a face like a Cherokee chief flourishes her glass, sips, swallows, and gasps. Or the grapes are being poured into sarcophagi for treading, and it is time to leave Clay Perry's brilliantly culled photographic drama; reluctantly, while the glasses clink and the fifteen-syllable rhyming couplets whizz to and fro and the dancers kick up a dust. The bow keeps pace across the lyra-strings, random gun-fire joyfully explodes, and the last treaders take their turn at the vat.

PATRICK LEIGH FERMOR
MESSENIA, JUNE 1991

And yet how lovely in thine age of woe,
Land of lost gods and godlike men, art thou!
Thy vales of evergreen, thy hills of snow,
Proclaim thee Nature's varied favourite now:
Thy fanes, thy temples to thy surface bow,
Commingling slowly with heroic earth,
Broke by the share of every rustic plough:
So perish monuments of mortal birth,
So perish all in turn, save well-recorded Worth . . .
LORD BYRON,
CHILD HAROLD'S PILGRIMAGE

The map of Greece is littered with place names that evoke, for Westerners, the entire, still-pungent landscape of Western history. Between the three 'Greek' seas – the Ionian, the Aegean and the Sea of Crete – the bird's eye picks out Delphi, Athens, Knossos, Sounion, Dodona, Patmos, Rhodes and Corinth. Across this stony ground strode Saint Paul, Pericles, Alexander, and the king we call Minos. In the nursery, we first heard the names Odysseus, Penelope, Ajax, Helen, Menelaus and Cassandra. Here, on the map, we find today Mycenae and Ithaca, and all the other ports from which the heroes of the Trojan War set out. What is vanishing is not the 'Greece of the West', the plays and principles and proud history of Hellas. Instead, it is the mantle across the hoary shoulders – the culture enriched by the Dorians, the Athenians and Spartans, the Byzantines, the Vlachs and the Franks. It is, as well, the forests and the littorals, the endangered monk seal's habitat, the nests of the loggerhead turtle; it is the Greece whose many names are *not* etched so indelibly on our collective memory that is being eroded, by the onslaught of Western culture itself, by acid rain, by fire, and by neglect.

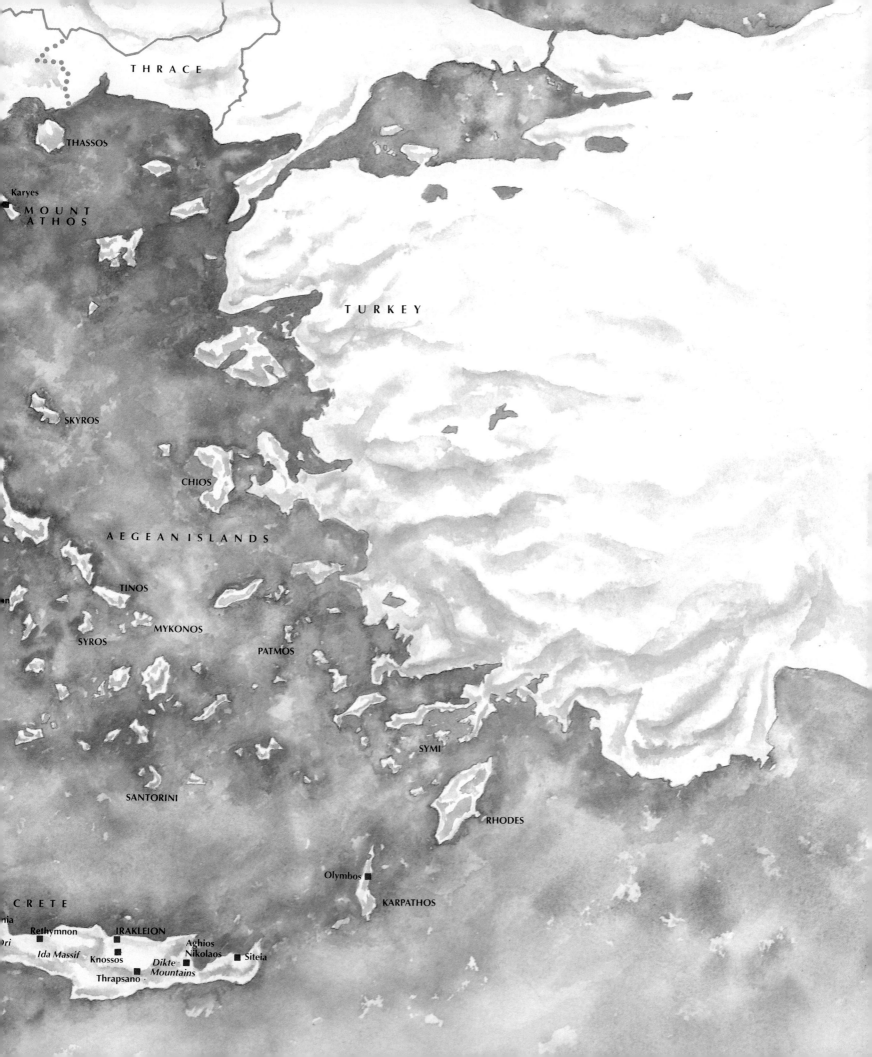

THRACE

THASSOS

Karyes

MOUNT
ATHOS

TURKEY

SKYROS

CHIOS

AEGEAN ISLANDS

TINOS

MYKONOS

SYROS

PATMOS

SYMI

SANTORINI

RHODES

Olymbos

KARPATHOS

CRETE

Rethymnon   IRAKLEION

Ida Massif

Aghios
Nikolaos
Knossos

Dikte   Siteia
Mountains

Thrapsano

THE MAINLAND

EPIRUS

EPIRUS IS THE CLOUD-COVERED CROWN OF GREECE, WEST OF the Ionian Sea, and the islands of Corfu, Paxi and tiny Andipaxi, and east of the long, rocky spine of the towering Pindus mountain range, the region's natural frontier with Thessaly. To the north is Albania, inhospitable and inscrutable behind an uneasy border frequently violated by the region's hardy Vlach and Sarakatsan shepherds and their flocks. The frontier has been crossed more recently and at great risk by ethnic Greek-Albanians fleeing the harsh regime of Tirana for an uncertain welcome in what they still hold to be their *patritha,* or fatherland.

Individualistic and fierce, Epirotes have always been people of the mountain, shifting between highland pastures and lowland dwellings according to the season. This rugged and, until very recent times, remote province, its mountain villages often inaccessible in winter, was home to Olympias, the indomitable mother of Alexander the Great; to Ali Pasha, the cunning and barbarous nineteenth-century 'Mohammedan Bonaparte'; to the Souliot women, who chose death before dishonour for themselves and their children in 1803; and, not last in a long list of controversial giants of history, to General Napoleon Zervas, commander of the Greek Resistance's guerrilla army, who fought the Germans, and then the communists in the stormy 1940s. It is no accident that to call someone an 'Epirot head' in Greece is to label him intractable, stubborn and proud. And today as well, despite the advent of electricity, running water and television soap operas, avidly watched in even the remote Zagorohoria, the characteristic villages of Zagori, Byron's description of the Epirot character, though it smacks of nineteenth-century chauvinism, still has some validity: Epirotes, he found in 1809, when he visited the Ali Pasha, were 'cruel, though not treacherous, and have several vices, but no meannesses. They are, perhaps, the most beautiful race, in point of countenance, in the world; their women are sometimes handsome also, but they are treated like slaves, beaten, and in short complete beasts of burden.' The truth of Byron's analysis lies in his estimation of Epirot resolve, stoicism and sense of honour, qualities in the people which have enabled them to deal with the rigours of their environment. Where nature showed no mercy, none was expected.

Even now, in the mountains, life is hard. Men are still termed *palikaria* (brave young warriors), and women *leventisses,* the female equivalent. A woman's lot continues to be harder and more constrained than a man's because of her double workload of domestic duties and agricultural toil. The hard existence is exacerbated by cruel winters spent in grim, depopulated villages, whose young people have been lured away to Ioannina, Athens and Frankfurt for work.

Epirus's traditional villages, and the traditional way of life mirrored in the arrangement of their structures, the activities and beliefs of their inhabitants, are fast becoming the stuff of legend, the stock of museums. Fortunately, keeping pace with the demise of villages and village life, with the 'embourgeoisement' of communities, is an acute awareness on the part of the Epirotes, scholars and lay people alike, of their tremendous cultural value. As the straight flute, or *floyera,* becomes an anachronism it, and its music, are being documented and preserved for prosperity. As villagers leave the Zagorohoria for the last time, descending to the warm lowlands that promise an easier life, the Greek government is going in and creating living museums out of the stone and hewn-oak houses. In fact, one plan has been proposed that would make the entire region of Zagori a sort of rustic theme park, to which admission would be charged.

The mountainous terrain of Epirus, crossed diagonally from north-northwest to south-southeast by four great ranges, whose limestone peaks rise to heights of over 1,828 metres (6,000 feet), comprises almost a quarter of the total area of mainland Greece, excluding the Peloponnese. In fact, Epirus means just that: 'mainland', or 'the continent'. Here, Greeks felt the land was solid beneath their feet, permanent, a certainty never vouchsafed to the islanders on their vulnerable, sea-bound perches, at the mercy of corsair and crusader. In the mountains of Alpine Epirus, Stone- and Bronze-Age Greeks and Albanians, and their descendants, now separated by imposed borders, have found refuge from invaders of all stripes by melting into the vast forests of fir, beech, oak and black pine, sheltering in caves unknown to the enemy, be he Cro Magnon, Molossian, Turk or German.

Ioannina, 21 kilometres (13 miles) northeast of Dodona on Lake Pambotis, may have been in existence as early as the 6th century AD, but the city came into its own only with the occupation of Constantinople, the capital of Byzantium, by the Crusaders, or Franks, in 1204. Henceforth, Ioannina, or the city of St John, would be a centre of continued Greek resistance, an independent Byzantine state. Michael I Comnenos-Ducas of Epirus founded the Despotate of Epirus, whose governmental seat was Arta, and ceded Ioannina to Byzantine refugees. The city and its island became a thriving Christian centre, which held out against the Ottoman Turks until 1430.

The Ottoman occupation of Ioannina lasted 482 years, during which time the city's famous guilds flourished, and Christians and Jews, respected by the Moslems as monotheistic 'People of the Book', organized according to

LEFT
The humble monastery of Aghios Panteleïmonas, on the tiny islet off Ioannina in Lake Pambotis, seems an unlikely place for the mighty Ali Pasha to have met his death. But in the upper gallery, now a small, kitsch museum, guards are happy to show visitors the holes in the floorboards where bullets tore through, ending the life of 'the worst unhung criminal in Europe.' It was in January of 1822 that the beseiged Albanian despot, along with a dozen of his faithful followers, and Vassiliki, 'the coiner's daughter of Plichivitza' who became his Christian wife, retired to the island. They were fleeing Khurschid Pasha, who was demanding Ali's unconditional surrender. The Sultan hoped that, with Ali's death, the Greek resistance movement would also die out, and the beleaguered ruler displayed Ali's head in Constantinople to prove without doubt that the Epirot insurrection was over. Ali Pasha was a figure of almost mythological stature. Chimerical and barbarous, he showed no mercy to his adversaries. No means were too violent for him, no deception too dishonourable in his drive for absolute power in the region. Yet he was a man of great personal charm, when it suited his ends. Capable of committing atrocities such as the drowning of Frossyni, his son's Greek mistress, and a group of other leading Christian women of Ioannina, several pregnant, Ali could also dazzle a Lord Byron, sending him 'almonds and sugared sherbet, fruit and sweetmeats, twenty times a day' and begging him 'to visit him often, and at night when he was at leisure.' Before he died, this 'petty chieftan from Tepeleni' had succeeded in establishing a semi-independent potentate and capturing the romantic Greek imagination, becoming the unlikely hero of scores of ballads and folk poems.

profession or trade. Even now, Ioannina retains some of this atmosphere of a guild town. The main commercial street is still lined with silversmiths, for Ioannina was once famous for its filigree and niello work, and the tradition persists. The capital, and Epirot villages in the Pindus such as Syrako and Kalarites, became known for their master jewellers.

Working in *lagara,* the purest silver, the jewellers of Ioannina created for Epirot ladies massive three-piece buckles, intricate bodice ornaments and heavy, jewelled headpieces worn on scarves at the temples. In these communities so dependent on flocks of sheep and goats, St George, patron saint of shepherds, was a frequent motif, as were the Virgin Mary and Christ. In Ioannina, niello work was most characteristic. Called *savati* in Greek, it is a technique that involves the filling of carved intaglio designs on silver or gold pieces with a mixture of powdered silver and lead, the proportions of which were always a closely guarded secret. When a piece is fired, a glossy black design on a silver base results. *Savati* and filigree work were sought-after additions to the dowries of Epirot brides from all over the region up through the nineteenth century. The old techniques have not died out and traditional designs are enjoying a renaissance, though orders for dowry pieces are long a thing of the past.

In Epirus, as throughout Greece, traditional culture, and all its time-tested forms, is disappearing faster than modern culture can find values, rituals and an alternative system of belief to replace the old, complex fabric of being. But the Greeks have a lively, informed sense of their ancestral ways, and there is a determined scholarly community of Greek and foreign archaeologists, anthropologists, linguists, musicologists, folklorists and lay people stepping into the breach to capture, on film, in museums, and in academic and popular literature, a way of life marked for extinction.

In the dramatically beautiful region of Zagori, or Zagoria, high in the Pindus mountains, intrepid visitors will still find vast, untouched Mediterranean forests. Above the timber line, sub-alpine grasses alone thrive in the cold, thin soils on bare, snow-dotted peaks. Fir and oak forests give way to sweeping alpine meadows, heavily grazed by flocks of goats and sheep. Away from the herds, beech forests thrive and, near the Aspropotamos River, mixed forests of beech, fir and black pine flourish. Here, on the Voïthomatis River, which cuts through the Vikos Gorge in a fierce flood of turquoise, plane trees and saplings shade the forest floor.

The Voïthomatis, or 'Ox-eyed One' River rushes past the foot of the Vikos Gorge cliff face. Attached like a stylite atop the rock perches the little monastery of Aristi Spiliotissa, the Exalted Virgin of the Cave. Here cherry trees blossom in spring. In summer their fruit tempts the European brown bear to descend from higher ground. The chamois and wolf are also infrequent visitors. The *Sus scrofa*, or wild boar, is sighted more often, and the Egyptian vulture soars in the clear air above the deep chasm. Monasteries here, such as Aghia Paraskevi and Aghios Athanasios, are being lovingly renovated in authentic Zagorian style, and the villages of the Zagorohoria are coming alive again after a century of decline, as the sons and daughters of Zagorians come to realize they have a unique cultural heritage worthy of preservation. Travelling through the 40-odd villages lying between Ioannina, Konitsa and the Albanian border, one traverses some of the most spectacular scenery in Europe. In fact, according to mountaineer Konstantinos Vassiliou, the Vikos Gorge is the largest in Europe, and Sheep's Gulf, where the Vikos Gorge bisects the Gamila massif, with its absolute vertical of over 400 metres (1,312 feet), is the world's second highest sheer drop.

'During these days time passed rapidly away, for there was full employment for every hour; one moment I would sit on the hill which rises west of the city, whence the great mountain of Mitzikeli on the eastern side of the lake is seen most nobly: at another, I would move with delight from point to point among the southern suburbs, from which the huge ruined fortress of Litharitza, with many a silvery mosque and dark cypress, forms exquisite pictures: or watch from the walls of the ruin itself, the varied effects of cloud or sunbeam passing over the blue lake, now shadowing the promontory of the kastron or citadel, now gilding the little island at the foot of majestic Mitzikeli...I was never tired of walking out into the spacious plain on each side of the town, where immense numbers of cattle enlivened the scene, and milk-white storks paraded leisurely in quest of food: or I would take a boat and cross to the little island, and visit the monastery, where that most wondrous man Ali Pasha met his death...'

EDWARD LEAR

On the little island in the lake, restaurants now vie for customers who are ferried over from Ioannina by motor launch. Live trout, eels, crayfish and frogs swim in tanks from which visitors may select their dinners, then sit by the waters of the lake, feeding ducks and swans that glide in the tiny harbour full of working watercraft. Primitive boat-building works still operate on the island, lone masters bending planks over fires to temper the wood. But Lake Pambotis and the Kalamas River, which feeds it, are threatened by pollution from fertilizers, pesticides and waste. The fisherman rowing in his handmade craft, and the trout, eels and crayfish, may soon become history. Nicoletta Kokkinou, who has lived in Ioannina all her life, says, 'the local people used to do their washing in the lake, it was so clean.'

TOP The Zagorian Plakidas Bridge, near Kipi, was originally built in 1814 by a monk named Serapheim and has been repaired twice: first in 1865/6 by Alex and Andreas Plakidas, and secondly in 1912, by Evghenios Plakidas, in memory of his father. Its three graceful arches connect the village of Koukouli, an hour to the north, with Asprangeli and Elati. The bridges of the Zagori region are masterpieces of form and are perfectly constructed. Built in the eighteenth century by the *Kioproulides,* or guilds of master craftsmen, they are made primarily of stone.

ABOVE LEFT Villages like Papingo provided a *himathia,* or winter refuge, for the shepherds and settled Sarakatsani, the former *Skinites,* or tent-dwellers. Papingo flourished during the thirteenth century and in various later periods after the Turkish conquest, though its church of Aghios Vlassis dates from the year 912. Today, the villages of Megalo and Mikro Papingo, on the slopes of Mount Timfi, lie within the territory of the protected Vikos-Aoös National Park.

LEFT The Boundaris Quarter in Megalo, or 'Big', Papingo, is where courtyard gates and unplastered stone walls line the stone-paved lane. Here, as throughout the area, dwellings were built on hillsides, rather than on precious level ground.

OPPOSITE ABOVE *'Eupolis, a contemporary of Aristophanes, wrote a comedy which he titled* The Goats. *Unfortunately, it has not survived, but we do know that it contrasted the quiet life of a goatherd with hectic city life. Two and a half millennia ago Eupolis's play favoured the goatherd's bucolic environment to that of Periclean Athens. Today still, goats graze the slopes of Mounts Pendeli and Parnes, high above sprawling, polluted, modern Athens. Time waits for no man, but for goats it stands still.'*
WILLIAM REID

OPPOSITE BELOW Each element of the bridal costume of the Sarakatsanissa had a name, and its exact composition and design was prescribed. One glance at a Sarakatsan bride could tell whether she hailed from Thrace or Epirus. In the components of this young girl's costume, handed down from her grandmothers, we can read the demise of the Sarakatsan as a living culture. She wears an authentic *kendisto katasarci,* or embroidered vest, but over a modern red pullover. The *kathimerinisca kapa,* or short cape, ends where the distinctive *brumanika,* or geometrically patterned sleeves begin. The *flora fustani,* or pleated, *foustanella*-like skirt, completes her costume. Here, the heir of the Sarakatsani and his daughter retain bits and pieces of an identity which seemed, only half a century ago, too vivid to be domesticated, let alone eradicated.

LEFT Sheep grazing on the high meadows near Kipi in spring. *'Another reason why sheep rearing will go on is that there are some who experience a* meraki *or yearning; this life has been in the blood for so long that a few will feel compelled to continue with it. To regret the decline in nomadic life for its own sake would be sentimental…'*
M. EVANGELOS AVEROF-TOSITSAS

'Metsovo, or Amintshu in the Vlach language which is still widely spoken, is divided into two parts. The larger, which is the administrative centre, is called Prosilio in Greek ("towards the sun") and Serinu by the Vlachi (meaning "sunny" from the Latin word serenus) and the smaller part, a scattering of houses far below at the foot of the valley where the Arakthos flows, is called Anilio (meaning "sunless") or Nkiare in Vlach (meaning "sunset").'

ARTHUR FOSS

In the main square of Metsovo, few of the elderly gentlemen sitting in the sun outside the kafeneia and souvlaki shops still wear the old, hobnailed and black pom-pomed tsarouchia, part of the age-old Vlach and Sarakatsan costume. Only one man now wears the black kilt, or foustanella, white wool leggings and black cap. For the other men, the shepherd's crook is primarily symbolic of a fast-disappearing pastoral life than of any living tradition. But the Vlachi still call Metsovo, 56 kilometres (35 miles) northeast of Ioannina, their capital. Located beneath the Katara Pass, on the

route between Meteora and western Epirus, this has long been an important site for shepherds, and has been made rich by wealth derived from the flocks. While the old fellows on the square are happy to direct visitors to the stunning Tositsa family mansion, now a museum of Epirot life and art forms, and the thriving Metsovo Folk Cooperative, which still produces the famous Metsovitiko wood carvings, embroideries, weavings and brass work, they will also caution you about wolves down in the valley near the fourteenth-century monastery of Aghios Nikolaos. The older

residents of Metsovo and environs may be difficult to understand, as *Vlachika,* their language, is not Greek at all, but a Romance language, Latin-based and reminiscent of Romanian. Traditionally transhumant shepherds, unlike the Greek-speaking Sarakatsani, who were true nomads, the Vlachi may have been trained by the Romans in ancient times for guard duty on the Via Egnatia, the main route from Constantinople to the Adriatic. Subsequent isolation in the high Pindus preserved their version of Latin, and with it their transhumant way of life.

The folk adage, *'Etsi ta mathameh keh etsi ta afinoumeh,'* or 'That's how we learned it and that's how we leave it,' is no longer valid in the Zagorohoria, the villages of Zagori. This old woman's home, wherein every stitch on coverlet, cushion and tablecloth, every woven rug and runner, was made by her and her alone, is a fine relic of another age, another age's values. The bridal overdress here, made by the old woman's grandmother, is a sleeveless *flokata* of the *sigouni* type. It would have placed the young bride as a Zagorian, 50 years ago when she married her young shepherd bridegroom. Made of thick, black wool, the *flokata* was 'ornamented with red ribbons, panels of red felt and embroidered patterns of red twisted cord. The two rectangular panels of red felt at the sides of the overdress are called *spatela.'* Says scholar Ioanna Papantoniou, 'The costume has its roots in tradition and is fundamentally different from what is "fashionable" dress, which is constantly affected by change. The conservative character of the costume favours the development of restrictive taboos, some of which attribute "magical" properties to certain components of the attire…' This woman, seated on her bed, proudly displaying her bridal *flokata,* lives in a village now deserted by all but three old women. In winter, all three retire to the relative comfort of life in Ioannina, when the Zagori is snowbound and inaccessible, but return in spring. Their granddaughters, living on the plains below, choose wedding dresses from the windows of bridal shops, and only such institutions as the Dora Stratou Foundation in Athens, retain the old sewing skills.

'...the best-known shoes in Greece are the tsarouchia, a type with upturned end decorated with a pompom. The original name of these shoes was pinges, and the most developed form, called mastorika or prokadoures, has the sole studded with nails and a large pompom on the upturned fore part.'
IOANNA PAPANTONIOU

Here, Vasilleios Stavrakis, a cobbler in Metsovo since 1915, works on a pair of heeled, tooled tsarouchia, still part of the daily costume of a few elderly Vlachi, and a treasured part of modern costumes assembled by young Metsovites, to be worn primarily during feast-day celebrations and village dances. The tiny red-leather tsarouches in Stavrakis's window are made for tourists and their key-rings, but the

shoe endures as a national symbol, and the heavy, hobnailed slippers are still worn by the honorary evzone guard outside the presidential palace in Athens.

In Greece, footwear speaks volumes, and is still today an almost infallible indicator of social standing. In the Greek shadow puppet theatre, it is Babayiorghos, 'Old Uncle George', the archetypal symbol of manly Greece, who wears the tsarouchia.

Ioannina, from the beginning of the nineteenth century, and into the twentieth, had a bustling commercial district which stretched from Aghios Nikolaos to the present Averof Street. As a 'typical eastern bazaar', it contained a dizzy variety of workshops. 'In its centre and around the mosque were candle-sellers, textile merchants and jewellers. On its periphery were the saddlers, coppersmiths,

blacksmiths, sellers of fresh produce, and around its entrances, the inns.' This *ganotis,* or tinsmith, practises a centuries-old tradition of fine craftsmanship that endures in the Epirot capital. With his polythene turban, this modern artisan harks back to the time of Ali Pasha, and his street and shop have changed little since the days of the despot. Like certain small areas of Monastiraki and Psiri in Athens, the bazaar in Ioannina has

escaped destruction, partly due to the spirit of mercantile individualism which has preserved one-man shops and the passing down of skills from father to son and, rarely, to daughter.

Greeks have always taken great pride in fine craftsmanship, in mastering and practising a manual skill. Long subject to masters *not* of their own choosing, they prefer to work alone in one-man businesses, answerable to themselves alone.

Next door to the tinsmith is the bakery, where Ioanniot bakers produce not only the *horiatiko psomi*, or village bread, and *frantzoles*, long, white loaves, favoured by modern housewives, but also *paximathia*, rusks, and speciality breads and biscuits, plus feast- and holy-day breads. In the morning, women with large families to cook for, arrive with their *tapsia*, huge round or rectangular baking tins, full of lamb and potatoes or *pastitsio*. The Ioannina bakers' guild is still the most powerful union in Greece, and almost all of the country's bakers are members. Until very recently, one would find non-Ioanniot bakers only in remote, undesirable locations of the country and, chances are, even today in Athens or Thessaloniki, the local baker will be from Epirus. Bread remains the staff of life throughout Greece. Villagers without a baker will divulge the fact with some shame.

In these similar-looking stone shops in the bazaar of Ioannina, with characteristic *fistique,* or pistachio-coloured woodwork, religious icons and *ta panta,* or 'everything', are offered for sale. In 1812, Henry Holland, writing of Ioannina, noted that:

'The Bazaars form the most interesting part of the city. They consist of ten or twelve streets, intersecting each other at irregular angles; very narrow, and still further darkened by the low, projecting roofs.'

Though very few of Ioannina's narrow mercantile streets are now still closed to motorized traffic, a few vestiges of the oriental bazaar have held out. Here, you will see signs written in *katharevousa,* tiny shops selling only knives, or tackle, or foul weather gear for shepherds and farmers, and even tinier shops carrying fine needlework for dowries. The gentleman offering *ta panta* features olive oil from Kalamata, the handle-less brooms preferred by elderly Greek women, who did not see broom handles till the late 1960s, and all sorts of scrubbing brushes for the cleanliness-obsessed *nikokyres,* or housewives. Some shops here are no larger than broom-cupboards. Throughout Greece the traditional general stores and tiny specialist shops are sadly dying out.

box containing the couple's wedding wreaths, or *stefana,* the fragile crowns of white which link marriage partners for life in the Greek Orthodox wedding ceremony.

LEFT Ioannina's walled and fortified Old Quarter, the Kastro, was the site of the original Byzantine town, settled by Christians fleeing the destruction of Constantinople, and was afforded vested rights of autonomy and many additional rights by two Gold Bulls issued by Andronicus II Paleologus in 1319 and 1321. Seized by the Turks in the early seventeenth century, the Kastro was then barred to all Christians, who settled outside the walls or emigrated abroad. The Moslems within the walls maintained fine homes with an upper floor, including three *sarayia,* mansions belonging to the Turkish officials. Two mosques, the Fetiche and Aslan Pasha, were magnificent structures. The Aslan Pasha, today being renovated, houses Ioannina's municipal museum, though the minaret is inhabited solely by rooks and is no longer accessible to visitors. Epirot master craftsmen, all guild members, erected the houses and mansions, many of which are still standing in and outside the Kastro. Specialized artisans, wood carvers and painters from Epirus's 'craftsmen villages' in the area of Konitsa worked on structures in the capital and fanned out to undertake construction contracts throughout Greece. So specialized was their knowledge that they spoke a private language known as *koudaritika,* and the Ioanniot mansions that did not succumb to fire in the nineteenth century bear witness to the skill of these builders. The spare facades facing the street with their projecting grill-work bely rich interiors with carved wooden and painted ceilings, fireplaces with plaster reliefs and intricate handmade weavings. In these alleyways, everything personal is hidden away behind silent, sealed doors.

LEFT A shop selling votive lamps and icons seems out of place in post-Byzantine Ioannina, but the custom of maintaining family icons persists, and a Greek house without its icons is not considered a home. In rural areas, the women of the house still light an oil lamp, or switch on an electric bulb resembling an oil lamp, in front of the family icons at dusk. They then pray to the Virgin or specific saints to look after the house and its residents through the night. Each house has its own ikonostasis, where the icons of the family's patron saints are housed. Usually attached to a bedroom wall, the ikonostasis may hang next to the

ROUMELI

ROUMELI IS NOW, AND HAS BEEN SINCE THE FIFTEENTH century, when the word was coined, a state of mind, rather than a state; a condition, rather than a country; a borderless place of exile, rather than a fatherland. Roumeli has never been a Greek word, yet it is a word all Greeks know. It is, as well, a term so fraught with meaning that to ask an elderly resident of *Ellatha,* the Greeks' own word for Modern Greece, what Roumeli means, is to elicit a long, impassioned tirade on *xenitia*—the state of displacement and longing experienced by Greeks alone.

As a word and as a geographical concept, however poorly defined, Roumeli came into being when the Turks took Constantinople in 1453, turning the Greeks out of Aghia Sophia, and converting the centre and symbol of Greek Orthodoxy, the holiest church in the world, into a mosque. It was the Turks who named the Greeks' *diaspora,* rubbing salt in the bitterest of wounds. Roumeli, in a sense, is the moral high ground the Greeks will inhabit until the realization of their 'Grand Idea', the *Megali Ithea* scoffed at by the young. Like the Jews, Greeks of a certain age believe Istanbul, like Jerusalem, has not been lost forever. It is still the country's spiritual capital.

Today Roumeli must be regarded as the mainland territory defined by the Greek War of Independence (1821–1833), an area delineated not by the Greeks, but by the protecting powers: England, France and Russia. The northern frontier, to the west of Epirus, and beneath Thrace, Macedonia and Thessaly, land that was still controlled by the Ottomans in 1928, stretches from the Gulf of Arta to the Gulf of Volos. To the south, Roumeli ends where the Peloponnese, or the Morea, begins, and rests upon the thin blue line of the Corinthian Gulf. Labelled by the Turks, fought for by the Greeks, and defined by the superpowers, the region contains those ancient sites so redolent of classical Greece: Thebes, Orhomenos, Thermopylae, Delphi, Athens and Sounion. Roumeli corresponds, roughly, to the contemporary governmental district known as *Sterea Ellatha,* or 'Solid Greece'. The district today is composed of five prefectures—Etolia/ Akarnania, Evritania, Fthiotida, Fokida, and Viotia—and within this wide belt of land, between Missolonghi and Lavrion, the Agrapha Mountains and Pelion, and Corinth to the south, there are ways of life as varied as any in the world.

PREVIOUS PAGE Thirty-one nautical miles southeast of Piraeus lies *Kavokolones,* or the 'Cape of the Columns', its cliff frosted with slender white Doric pillars, a sight familiar to all visitors leaving Piraeus for the Aegean isles. On the windy bluff above the sea stands the Temple of Poseidon, built in the fifth century BC, just when Pericles was beginning to erect the great Athenian structures on the Acropolis. Sounion's whiteness is due to the builder's use of Agrilezan marble, not Parian, which contains no iron and thus retains its brilliance over time, unlike Pentelic marble, which weathers to beige, pink or ochre. Mentioned by Homer in the *Odyssey* in the eighth century BC, Sounion was an important Attic sanctuary long before the erection of the classical temple. In fact, two temples shared the promontory in antiquity, the second dedicated to the goddess Athena, Poseidon's traditional rival. The bluff itself was sealed off by massive, fortified walls which protected barracks for a garrison, boathouses for Athenian warships, a stoa and storehouses. During the Peloponnesian War of 431-404 BC, the fort was strengthened in order to secure safe passage for Athenian ships off the headland. In decline since the first century BC, when the Temple of Athena was dismembered and moved to the Agora, Sounion was no longer a hallowed site. When that 'First Tourist', the Roman travel writer Pausanius, sailed by and described Sounion in the second century AD, he wrongly identified the remains of Poseidon's Temple as Athena's, a misconception that endured through Byron's day. Today, tour coaches park at the foot of the hill beneath the sanctuary, but visitors are barred from entering the temple, which is roped off. Eighteenth- and nineteenth-century graffiti, including Byron's signature, have disfigured the columns, and the inscriptions are written in every European language, including Greek.

Here are primitive mountain villages, where a daughter who elopes may still be shot dead by her father; ascetic monastic retreats atop islands of rock stranded on an alluvial plain; Athens, an urban capital which has drained the country dry of a third of its population, and whose classical monuments are now dissolving in a bath of acid rain; traditional settlements preserved by the State; and traditional settlements long become ghost towns whose farming implements belonging to departed shepherds have been removed to Athenian museums.

Here, too, are Greece's next most famous mountains after Olympus: Hymettus, Penteli, and Parnitha. All three are celebrated in classical poetry and song, but now ring Athens in a deadly bowl from which Europe's worst blanket of smog, the *Nefos,* cannot escape. Home to resistance fighters in the wars against the Turks, these three peaks today ensure the city's slow demise, and the simultaneous disintegration of the Periclean temples on the Acropolis, symbols, for the entire Western world, of the legacy of Ancient Greece. In Athens, measures are being taken to control car and industrial emissions and preserve the marbles, as the Greeks are only too aware of what they stand to lose.

The Meteora, in Thessaly, and Pelion, the mountainous region near Volos, are two areas above the brow of Roumeli proper which are also experiencing a timely renaissance in the late twentieth century, their traditions reviving; their characteristic architecture and ways of life being preserved.

The Meteora consist of more than 20 perpendicular rocks located on the western edge of the plain of Thessaly above the little village of Kastraki. Here, the Pinios River emerges from the high Pindus onto the Thessalian plain, an area which, according to Herodotus, was once submerged beneath a vast inland lake whose only egress to the sea was via the Vale of Tempe far to the east. Composed of stratified conglomerate, the weathered grey 'stalagmites', for so they appear, as if standing in some vast, illuminated cave, rise sheer, hundreds of metres above the village's red-tiled roofs. The rocks give way at their very pinnacles to the stone and plaster walls of dizzily-perched monasteries which are often obscured from sight in spring and winter by low-lying fog and cloud.

Off season, when Kastraki empties of tourists, and only the villagers, monks, and nuns stay on, the former going about their seasonal work in the fields below, the latter at prayer in the monasteries above, the entire area of the Meteora seems to regress in time. Few cars disturb the peace, though this is the time of year when monastic brothers and sisters from other retreats come to visit, and road signs request one and all, in several languages, to respect the region's sanctity. Dogs, donkeys and roosters are exempt from this ruling, and barnyard sounds repeatedly ricochet off the rock faces in an eerie cacophony. The topography of Kastraki itself is punctuated by fragile-looking needles of stone, and by women bending in fields beneath a chapel midway up a cliff. Tucked like a piton in the rock is the tiny Chapel of St George of the Kerchief, festooned with bright pennants like some crazy, mid-air sailing ship.

The northern European mountaineers who climb the Meteora with ropes and rock hammers are this secular century's answer to the monks who first scaled the rocks in the ninth century. The first anchorites, or hermits, who ascended the needles were in headlong flight from the world. Varnavas, who founded the Retreat of the Holy Spirit sometime between AD 950 and 965, and Andronikos of Crete who, in 1020, built a hermitage on the rock which today supports the Monastery of the Transfiguration, were the first to come. Other monks from all over Byzantium followed, swelling the number of the monastic houses to 24. Reaching the height of its importance in the seventeenth century, the community has been in decline ever since. Today, six of the monasteries, one inhabited by nuns, are still open, but a recent increase in the ranks of monks throughout the Orthodox world, coupled with a concern, on the part of both Church and State, that such treasures as the monasteries of the Meteora must not be allowed to decay, have ushered in a quiet religious resurgence atop the silent pinnacles.

Across the vanished Thessalian seabed, Mount Pelion rises some 1,635 metres (5,364 feet) above the Aegean Sea, and well-watered slopes forested with pines, oaks, fir trees, wild olives and chestnuts plunge down to glorious pristine beaches. This green peninsula embracing the Pagasitikos Gulf was known in the twelfth century as 'the second Mount Athos', because so many monasteries were built here. The monastic enclaves attracted Vlach serfs and monk-farmers, drawn by word of the monasteries' rich, fertile and protected holdings. Agricultural production remained the staple of the economy during the *Tourkokratia*, but silk became an increasingly important product, and it was sericulture, the manufacture of thread, weaving and tanning, which ensured Pelion's great prosperity in the eighteenth century. Ironically, it was the waves of nineteenth-century revolution, culminating in Thessaly's annexation by Free Greece in 1881, which spelled the end of Pelion's ascendancy.

The rich merchant villages, studded with characteristic mansions, schools, churches, monasteries, shady squares, fortified towers and silk factories constituted a distinct cultural entity as unique as that of Ioannina in Epirus, the Mani in the Peloponnese, or Kastoria in Macedonia, but they fell victim to the changing economic and political climate of the modern world. The rich interweave of Pelion culture required an influx of capital to maintain it, and the great homes were disintegrating just as the trend to preserve Greece's folk heritage came into its own in the 1970s.

Until the middle of the twentieth century, Pelion's legacy, and the Meteora, along with the Acropolis marbles, were threatened. Of late, private initiatives mounted by the descendants of Magnesia's great families, as well as the Greek government, are coming to the rescue of such villages as Pelion's Vizitsa and Milies. The Meteora, supported by their holdings of land and timber, the Church, and now, foreign visitors as well, are holding their own. Least certain is the future of the great, exposed marbles; but they, in a very real sense, are the responsibility of us all.

These rocks rise tormented
Like the Byzantine soul to the sky.
Wounded obelisks, beast of a
granite
Nightmare, towering cubes and
tablets
Fit for the Ten Commandments to
be carved upon,
They move disdainful away
From the ashen, pestilent plain.
Monasteries cling to their tops,

Deserted in a world that has
forgotten
How to pray, suspended
Far from the warm flowers of
spring
In the sad fight of man to trample
His flesh—the look
In the upturned eyes of ascetics
And saints on their pale, fading
frescoes.

C.A. TRYPANIS

The spiritual aim of Orthodox Christian life is the acquisition of the Holy Spirit. The monk and nun spend every moment of the day in constant effort to draw closer to God. Aware that, in the words of Macarius of Egypt, the human heart is 'the workshop of good and evil,' they are concerned with purifying their natures, perfecting their spirits. Since union with God can only be achieved through prayer, the ascetics of the Meteora have withdrawn from the world in order to pray ceaselessly. Suspended between heaven and earth, the nearby town of Kastraki is often hidden from them beneath the clouds. The inhabitants of the monasteries were once able to seal themselves off from the distractions and temptations of temporal reality, but today, the many uninhabited and ruined monasteries and *sketes*, primitive 'swallows' nests' inhabited by lone hermits, bear witness to the decline of monasticism as a vocation. Still, the remaining anchorites observe a strict regimen, and visitors are allowed in on certain days only, and their attire is subject to very specific rules of propriety.

The temple at Delphi is as awe inspiring today as it was to the ancient pilgrims. It was said to have been discovered by Zeus, who, wishing to find the precise centre of the world, loosed two sacred eagles from the ends of the earth. They met above Delphi, henceforward known as the *omphalos,* or world's navel. The Apollonian Oracle, whose priestess, or *Pythia,* delivered answers to queries put by supplicants, envoys of the rich and powerful, including kings, exercised unparalleled influence in the ancient world. From the eighth century BC onward, till her final utterance in the reign of Julian (AD361-362), she, and those who 'interpreted' her runic responses determined the course of history. Croesus, who sought her guidance before waging war on Persia, was told that if he proceeded with his plans he would destroy a great kingdom. He did, but the kingdom he destroyed turned out to be his own. Ancient, pagan Greece ended with the silencing of Apollo's priestess. When Julian sent emissaries to consult the oracle, he was answered by a priest:

'Say to the king: in ruin the once gay courts of the temple lie, not a shelter of boughs has the god, nor speaks in the laurel nor in the fountain; silent is even the voice of the water.'

'What is unique in Athens is the quality of Time: a thin, fine lucid element with a minimum of intervening literary connotations, and without the grey or gorgeous encrustations of a medieval period or Renaissance: a medium in which the historical sense of the inhabitants operates less as the result of conscious education or imaginative romance than simply as an unawareness of the passage of time itself—an almost primeval sense of the past as present. There is in fact, underneath the brassy ambitions of the modern city, very little to obstruct a view back to the populous intricacies of the ancient world—very little between today and the undifferentiated millennium of Frankish and Byzantine Athens, or between ourselves and the torpid frightened yesterday of Turkish centuries or even the quiet peppery provincial gracefulness of Athens up to the Second World War.'

KEVIN ANDREWS

The Acropolis temples, lit by the apricot and violet Attic half-light, with purple Mount Hymettus in the background, are the enduring symbol of Periclean Athens, and the Golden Age of Greece. Erected between 447 and 438 BC, and financed by slave labour in the rich silver mines of Lavrion, the buildings remained largely intact for some two thousand years before removals, first by the Romans and, subsequently, by self-serving eighteenth- and nineteenth-century 'collectors', plus a mortar attack by a Swedish mercenary (26 September 1687), put an end to the perfection envisaged by Pheidias, Iktinos and Kallikrates, the fifth century architect and sculptors. Built to replace earlier Acropolis temples razed by the Persians, and to symbolize the city's rebirth from the ashes, the Parthenon was dedicated to Athena. Constructed of Penteli marble, quarried on the mountain northeast of the capital, the Doric temple is a masterpiece of optical illusion.

ABOVE AND RIGHT In Vizitsa, on the western slopes of Mount Pelion, the Kondos Mansion, built in 1792, has been restored to its former glory and turned into a working inn by the Greek National Tourist Organization. Most of Pelion's present-day villages, now reviving as a result of an influx of tourism, were true eighteenth-century 'cities', thriving centres of the silk trade. Pelion's rich market towns enjoyed self government and independence from Ottoman Turkey. The mansions of wealthy Pelion families were amply fortified. In the Kondos Mansion, for example, a pipe connects the kitchen with a portal above the entrance from which boiling oil could be poured on intruders. The fortified dwellings built during Pelion's heyday, between 1750 and 1830, embody architectural elements gleaned from both East and West. The Thessalian tradition is represented in the tower-like stone base of the houses, and the projecting upper storeys, but the 'form' of the interiors mirrors the Orient. Pelion's structures also reflect more local influences, and the 'rules' of the Balkans and the Ottomans were bent to Pelion's needs. Here, the unceilinged *sala*, or reception space, in the Kondos Mansion's top-storey summer residence hall, illustrates the refinement of Pelion's eighteenth-century lifestyle.

TOP RIGHT Pelion's villages, unconnected by paved roads till this century, depended and depend on ponies, mules and donkeys. In the mountain villages, hooved transport moves firewood, groceries and building timber. The packsaddler and farrier are still valued citizens in such hamlets as Milies. The muleteers, busy transporting materials to rebuild Pelion in the 1940s and 1950s kept local saddler Vanghelis Katartzis working day and night. Today, there are comparatively few animals on the mountain, Katartzis makes few new saddles, but finds he repairs many old ones.

CENTRE RIGHT The Pelian squares are the settlements' most interesting feature. Says architect Rea Leonidopoulou-Stylianou:

'The particular characteristics of each composition, the general shape, size and position in space are projected so strongly that the image of most villages is identified with the image of their square.'

The public areas evolved from flat threshing floors, positioned to facilitate the exhibition of products and the exchanges transacted by agricultural communities. Small cemeteries, as well, might be transformed into squares. Attended by churches, from which all the festivals, public and more private, of Pelion life spilled, these areas were ideally suited to fulfill a brighter role in village life. On Pelion's squares, religious, economic, social and administrative functions found a stage. Here were, and are, the revered, shady plane trees set like islands of repose in the flagstone paving, the public fountain, the *kafeneion,* and the moderns' answer to the ancients' theatre.

BELOW RIGHT *'The "Renaissance" influences, which the rich merchant owners received from their contact with Europe, are obvious, both in the organization of the spaces and the decoration of the houses.'*

REA LEONIDOPOULOU-STYLIANOU

MOUNT ATHOS

'In the Corpus Eremiticum, *a work of the Early Fathers, there is the following story. Some strangers come to a hermit and ask him what experiences he has as a hermit. The man, who is in the course of fetching water from a cistern, draws up the bucket and asks the strangers to take a look down into the well. What do they see there? The strangers look into the depths and answer, "Nothing!" After a while the strangers look down once more into the depths; the hermit again puts his question, and this time the strangers answer, "Ourselves, our faces." The hermit says, "When I was busy, the well was restless. Now there is peace, and one can see what one is. That is the experience of being an anchorite."*

E. KAESTNER

Outside the Monastery of Stavronikita, a young monk in his *skoufos* and cassock gazes into the distance: to the east and south, there is nothing but sea. He is reflected in the still water of the elevated pond, where fish are raised to supplement the fathers' simple diet. Beside the pond is the seventeenth-century aqueduct which provides the monastery with water and, to the left, the characteristic, crennelated tower and buttressed upper storey of Stavronikita.

MOUNT ATHOS, AND THE ATHONITE MONKS, ARE suspended in amber, outside time as we know it. They are also outside Greece as we know it. Located on the easternmost of Chalkidiki's peninsulas, the three arthritic fingers of land that jut into the Aegean south of Thessaloniki and west of the island of Thassos, the Holy Mountain, or *Aghion Oros,* as it is known to the Greeks, is an autonomous part of the State. Like the Vatican, it is, in essence, a monastic republic. The government is based on rules and regulations laid down in the tenth, eleventh, fourteenth and nineteenth centuries, and reaffirmed by the constitutional charter of 1924. This latter document provides for a Holy Assembly, composed of one representative each from the 20 ruling monasteries. The assembly now meets twice annually in Karyes, the holy community's capital, where a separate committee of four overseers, equal in status and selected from the 20 houses on a rotating basis, in addition to a *Protoepistates,* or Chief Monk, determine the affairs of the inhabitants of Mount Athos.

When the peninsula was liberated from the Turks in 1912, the monastic population was 10,000, but the number of monks has varied throughout history, reaching an all-time low of 1,150 in 1972. This figure was never accepted as permanent, or as a cause for real worry by most Athonites, however. In the words of the Archimandrite Gabriel, speaking in 1956 as abbot of the Monastery of Dionysiou, 'The splendour and grandeur of the Holy Mountain is not to be judged by the small or large number of monks who dwell on it. This fluctuation has occurred many times during its thousand-year period of monastic life . . . We Aghiorites steadfastly believe that our holy abodes on Mount Athos will soon be filled with monks . . . We believe that the mountain, by the Grace of God, will continue in existence till the end of time.' Gabriel's faith, it seems, is being borne out. Athos's ranks are, indeed, swelling as, over the past decade, younger and better educated novices—though education is not seen as particularly beneficial to a monk's progress—are expressing a monastic vocation. It seems the Holy Mountain's insistence that the peninsula contains something of inestimable value is drawing more and more applicants to seek access to the monasteries, and the little medieval town of Karyes, through which all visitors must pass on their way to the monastic retreats, often has trouble accommodating the crowds.

At Karyes, as well as the administrative offices, is the seat of the civil governor, who answers to the Ministry of Foreign Affairs in Athens, and is assisted by a handful of officials and a token police force. But despite this nominal presence, Modern Greece seems impossibly distant and unreal on this densely wooded arm of land where the power grid and modern road system have not been permitted to intrude. From the civil boundary near the town of Ouranoupolis, the Holy Mountain is cut off, inviolable. Approximately 57 kilometres (35 miles) in length, and between seven and 10 kilometres (four to six miles) wide, the 389 square kilometres (150 square miles) of seabound land, dominated by the 2,000 metre (6,561 feet) high pyramid of Mount Athos itself, represents a latter day bastion of Byzantium. Visitors, and only male visitors with a vocation, may cross over for brief visits, and even they must run the bureaucratic and spiritual gauntlet before obtaining their 'passports'. Smoking, phonographs, long hair, video cameras, and even musical instruments, are forbidden.

At the offices of the Greek National Tourist Organization in Athens and Thessaloniki—and the initial permission to visit Athos may be granted in these two cities alone—modern pilgrims will be given a sheet of instructions, 'Regulations Concerning The Visiting of Mount Athos By Foreigners'. The list of prerequisites is daunting. Women are, of course, barred entry, and have been since the eleventh century, along with any 'eunuch, beardless person, female animal, or child'. Constantine IX's ruling regarding the beardless, and some female animals, has been relaxed, but women are not allowed within 500 metres (547 yards) of the shoreline. Even the volume of loudspeakers on passing pleasure craft is controlled by law.

To approach the Holy Mountain is, by definition, to embark on a personal pilgrimage. Written between the lines of the holy fathers' supervising entry, of course, is the hope, even the belief, that any visit, however casually conceived, will evolve into a pilgrimage. The stories of visitors who came to see Athos's famous libraries of illustrated manuscripts, its priceless frescoes, and portable icons chased in gold, later returning to become monks, are numerous. While safeguarding the precious *esychia,* or complete, spiritual quiet required for prayer and growth in God, the monastic leaders simultaneously ensure that only those who will appreciate the aims of Athos, the way of Athos, will gain admittance. Only he who believes in the Grail, they feel, can seize the Grail.

Ironically, the 'republic' closed to women is by no means misogynist. In fact, it may be said that the monks keep before them, throughout their day of action and of prayer, the idealized image of 'all woman', in the form of the Mother of God. According to one ancient tradition, the Virgin, accompanied by John the Evangelist, actually visited the Holy Mountain and claimed it as her own. For this reason, say the monks, all other women are banned. On her way to visit Lazarus on Cyprus, Mary's ship was carried off course by a storm and the Virgin put ashore near the present day Monastery of Iveron. Dazzled by the natural beauty of the rugged landscape, she asked her son to grant her the mountain as a gift. A voice responded saying, 'Let this place be your inheritance and your garden, a paradise and a haven of salvation for those seeking to be saved.' Mindful of the reason for mankind's expulsion from the original garden, the occupants of the second earthly paradise sought to secure their future. Not even flocks would be allowed to graze Mount Athos, and female birds alone would be permitted to challenge the Virgin's sovereignty. Chastity, second among the three monastic virtues, along with poverty and obedience, would be offered up to the Mother of God as a gift. Rather than shunning all women as inferior or corrupt, the monks, in a sense, exalt the female principal, aspiring to the virginity of the 'Ever Virgin Mother' herself. For Athonites, She is the key to *theosis,* to the metamorphosis of 'Man into God, God into Man'. In the pledge of chastity each ascetic makes to the Virgin, he states: 'She is my mother, sister, wife and daughter', the *Platitera Ton Ouranon,* or mantle upon which all Creation rests.

On the Holy Mountain, the mantle and cowl of monasticism represent much more than a simple renunciation of worldly attire. In putting on the habit, the monks put off the world, donning the spiritual armour required for a fierce and private lifelong battle with evil and temptation, both within and without. The monk's traditional clothing advertises his enlistment in an army with no ranks, no officers, no leader but Christ. In the words of St Ephraim, the monk's robe and cowl or, more commonly today, the *skoufos,* or conical hat, are worn to remind each humble brother of the gruelling spiritual work ahead. The rosary, given each novice upon his taking of monastic vows, becomes his 'spiritual sword'; his 'martial art' the art of prayer, which he will practice for up to ten hours a day till death. Through prayer, the monk hopes to gain admittance to God's presence, to stand before Him, in ceaseless conversation with the Creator.

Mount Athos has aspired to become God's workshop and the Virgin's garden for more than twelve centuries, and a host of saints, mystics and holy writers, throughout its long, unbroken history, attest to the ongoing validity of its monastic mandate. Even in the writings of this century, of artists, scholars and simple lay people who visit the Holy Mountain and then recount their experiences, the stories of miracles, conversions and moments of truth abound.

In *Report To Greco,* Nikos Kazantzakis's literary last will and testament, he recounts a meeting with a senile old sage on Athos, 'a half-insane ascetic' who lived 'perched in a cave overhanging the sea'. Kazantzakis, to tease the hermit says, 'Poor, poor man, I see you've lost your wits...' In true Athonite style the monk replies: 'I gave my wits and received God in return. In other words, I gave a counterfeit farthing and purchased paradise. What do you think, my boy, did I strike a good bargain?' Kazantzakis, 'muzzled', has no reply. 'After a moment's silence, the hermit continues. "And let me tell you something else, for your information. There was once a great king who had three hundred and sixty-five wives in his harem. He was very handsome, and loved to eat and have a good time. One day he went to a monastery, where he saw an ascetic. He looked at him compassionately. 'What a great sacrifice you are making!' he said. 'Your sacrifice is greater,' the ascetic replied. 'How's that?' 'Because I have renounced the ephemeral world, while you have renounced the eternal.'

PREVIOUS PAGE Behind the domes of the *Katholikon,* or main church, of the Monastery of Stavronikita, snow-capped Mount Athos floats in a palate of blue and green on the horizon.

RIGHT Seminary students from Karyes stand before the *Skete* of St Andrew, which belongs to the Monastery of Vatopedi. The site has a long and checkered history. Originally a small monastic house dedicated to St Anthony, the buildings were renovated in the seventeenth and eighteenth centuries by two patriarchs, who chose to live here. The second of these eminent benefactors, Serapheim II, erected a three-storey structure with a large chapel dedicated to St Andrew. Subsequently, the Turkish governor of Mount Athos requisitioned the monastery for his headquarters and, in 1842, St Andrew's, now a *kelli* (a smallholding consisting of a building, a chapel and some land, usually home to only three monks), was ceded to the Russian monk, Bessarion.

OPPOSITE TOP LEFT Standing on the steps of the *Hiera Koinotes,* the assembly hall of the Holy Community in Karyes, are two *seimenithes,* or members of the Athonite Guard, dressed in the white kilt, or *foustanella,* which was once the military uniform of Greece's revolutionary chieftans.

OPPOSITE TOP RIGHT Karyes is Mount Athos's administrative centre and only 'town'. Here in the Street of *Aghiou Pnevmatos,* or the Holy Spirit, Greek flags fly in the medieval streets, heralding a rare and historic visit by the Ecumenical Patriarch, Demetrius, from Constantinople.

OPPOSITE BOTTOM A brace of black-belted *monahi,* or monks, at their shop on *Aghiou Pnevmatos,* where religious souvenirs, all hand-made made by Athonites, are offered for sale.

'One day, while I roam St Panteleïmonas's dusky, abandoned corridors … I come across the Russian abbot. He is gazing, intently, from the top storey, out across the open expanse of the Sigitikos Gulf… "Look," he says in broken Greek. "It is from here that the Patriarch will come!" He is awaiting a miracle. I pity his poor, deranged delusions. He expects the Patriarch of Moscow after over half a century to come to reclaim the great, silent Russian monastery and to bring a new generation of Russian ascetics to revitalize the dying institution and, thus, begin the redemption of Holy Russia: to wrest his fallen, atheist motherland from the hands of the terrible Bolsheviks. "Miracles!" he whispers in his thick, barely intelligible Russian accent. "Miracles are the answer to prayer!" And he quotes St Paul: "Pray unceasingly!" … Suddenly, one day, I wake to clear skies… As I approach the little wharf of the Russian Monastery, I am shocked to see the abbot in his fine priestly vestments together with an assembly of Russian monks… Have the abbot's personal delusions now spread to others as well?… "Look," a Greek monk greets me. "We await the great Patriarch of Moscow!" And, sure enough, as if appearing from a cloud of salt spray, approaching our shore is a flotilla of caïques and Greek patrol boats. Flying aloft from their masts, along with the blue and white cross of the Greek flag, are innumerable Byzantine banners just like those carried by the Russian monks!… It is indeed Patriarch Pimen of Moscow, coming to reclaim the Monastery of St Panteleïmonas— hastening to initiate the repentence of Holy Russia and a new age of Athonite miracles. I was able to depart with the Patriarch. On our voyage back to Ouranoupolis…I reflected upon the lessons which the Holy Mountain still offers a world in rebellion against piety and faith.'
STEPHEN D. SALAMONE

TOP AND ABOVE High above the Aegean, Stavronikita stands like a compact little ship in space. One of the first monasteries in recent times to change over from an idiorrhythmic way of life, whereby the monks retain private property and matters of work and food are left to the individual, Stavronikita is now coenobitic, and everything is communal. In the refectory, decorated by fine murals executed by Theophanes the Cretan and his son Symeon, the monks share their common, vegetarian meals that are accompanied by wine.

OPPOSITE A monk circles the courtyard of Stavronikita striking a small, resounding wooden *semantron*, or gong, summoning the monks to vespers. In the words of Father Anthimios:

'It is said that Noah used the semantron *to call the animals into the Ark, and thus save them from the Deluge; and that following his example, we employ it to call the monks into church, which is a spiritual Ark, in order that they might be saved from the deluge of sin.'*

'Coming out from the first even-song, I went down to the beach and gazed at the waves, at the emerald hills, the blue shadow of an Aegean island opposite me, to free myself. It was a blessed sunset. The sea, somehow still, had so controlled her movement that it had become rhythmical. Distant her breath sounded, harsh, but ordered and joyful. In measured time the wave leapt and fell like snow, stirring the pebbles. A young monk came out alone to go for his walk on the deserted sands, after the even-song. His slender build, in his Byzantine dress, was very clearly outlined on the whiteness of the sand, in the sunset. He was still young. If he went back into the world, he would have, for good or evil, a human history. Here it was not possible. He was a monk. He would grow old, he would learn the texts by heart, he would die—that was his life.'
Z. PAPANTONIOU

At Stavronikita, as at the other 19 monasteries on the Holy Mountain, each of the monks works for his own monastic house. Due to the overall decline in numbers, monks may take on tasks formerly undertaken by several brothers, and lay labourers from nearby towns and islands may be hired seasonally to do work formerly assigned to monks alone. Here, a young monk dressed in his blue work clothes fetches a stray pony. As the *bordonaris,* or *chatlaris,* of Stavronikita, he is responsible for the monastery's livestock. Other monastic titles are assigned to such 'specialists' as the monastery's baker, the holder of the keys to the library, the monk in charge of a miracle-working icon and its chapel, and the gatekeeper and *koudonokroustis,* who beats the *semantron.* These are just some of the many divisions of labour on Mount Athos, where the monastic day falls into three distinct parts of eight hours each: one dedicated to prayer, one to work, and the final one to sleep.

OPPOSITE At Stavronikita, Father Demetrios lights a candle, and says a prayer to St Nicholas, patron of his monastery. Illuminated by the golden light of a beeswax candle is the mosaic icon of St Nicholas *Streidas,* or St Nicholas of the Oyster, housed in the *Katholikon.* Rescued by fishermen from the sea off Mount Athos, the icon was disfigured by an oyster, which had attached itself to the saint's forehead. It is said that when the oyster was removed, St Nicholas's head bled. Awash in the sea for 500 years, the icon is believed to have come from Constantinople, whence it fled upon the invasion by Ottoman Turks.

ABOVE In the refectory, a monk lights a gas lamp. Since Mount Athos is not on the national grid, and only a few monasteries maintain their own generators that are used only in winter, rooms are lit, when lit at all, by gas, kersosene, oil and candle-light. The 40-odd members of Stavronikita eat among frescoes of the Cretan School which depict the Last Supper. The periods of fasting to which the monks adhere are numerous and rigorous; amounting to more than 240 days of each year. At these times, fresh fish, eggs, cheese, other items of animal origin, and even oil and wine have no place in the diet.

LEFT *'A pot of basil may symbolize the soul of a people better than a drama of Aeschylus.'*
I. DRAGOUMIS

A sprig of basil is one of the traditional gifts of rural Greece. Here, at Stavronikita, a *Vassiliko,* or 'Kingly One', grows in a niche by a fresco of St George.

The juxtaposition of sweet-smelling herbs such as basil and mint, and icons is particularly Greek. On saints' days and at Easter, Orthodox Churches are filled with flowers and pungent greenery; the natural scents of the leaves and blossoms mingling with those of incense and beeswax.

LEFT AND BELOW Eclectic architectural elements, such as the Venetian marble fountain backing, the crimson bell tower atop the *Katholikon,* and the spacious courtyard, with its gazebo, spring, and independent chapels, bear witness to Iveron's long history of building and renovation. The monastery is a rich repository of precious gifts and treasures, including reliquaries, codices and portable icons. Most precious among these objects are the relics of some 150 saints, including the limbs of Basil the Great, and St Marina. The Athonites revere the relics of the Saints, believing they are capable of 'emitting remedies'.

ABOVE A courtier named John of Iberia (Russian Georgia) rejected his worldly life to found the Monastery of Iveron, or 'the Iberians'. Dedicated to the Dormition of the Virgin Mary, a chapel at Iveron houses a miracle-working icon of the Virgin *Portaïtissa,* or Mother of God Who Keeps the Gate. Said to have travelled for 70 years over the sea from Constantinople, this icon came to rest upon the site of the present monastery. Iveron is unique among Athonite houses because it uses the Chaldean clock, whereby sunrise is taken as twelve o'clock, and also because of its missionary work.

'The chanting at Iviron was very good. The articulation both of the right and the left chanters was distinct, the tempo was neither unduly fast nor too slow, and the voices were beautiful. A few compositions, such as the Cherubic Hymn, were sung slowly, as they are meant to be sung. No concession was made at this or the other Greek monasteries on Athos to Western music. The ancient Christian tradition of antiphonal, monophonic, purely vocal music, which was transmitted by the Byzantines, has been preserved.'
CONSTANTINE CAVARNOS

ABOVE 'The Holy Mountain is legally constituted as an independent, self-governing ecclesiastical state. Prior to the Second World War... It was tax-exempt, it was self-sufficient and without a trade deficit, and enjoyed an almost inexhaustible supply of cheap labour. Its territory was exceptionally fertile; indeed it was one of the few places in Greece where forests and large trees survived, and its estates were extremely well managed, their major production being in walnuts, wood, citrus fruits, olives, grapes, male livestock, handicrafts, and religious art.'
STEPHEN D. SALAMONE

RIGHT *'Boat-landing areas on Athos are often small ports, with now-abandoned living quarters and storage areas or "customs houses", and turreted watch towers. It is not unusual to see logs piled high on the jetties since some of the monasteries deal in timber, a major source of income. The caïque pulled in and we took our place beside several monks clutching plastic shopping bags containing the few items they would need on their journey. As the caïque passed close to the shore, tiny cells (skites) built into the cliffs came into view.'*
CHARLES McIVOR KOTSONIS AND JOHN HARALAMBOS LEWIS

A panoramic view of the kitchen gardens of the Monastery of Pantokrator, today an idiorrhythmic house which has occupied seventh place in the Athonite hierarchy since the late sixteenth century. Pantokrator and its dependencies are home to a present total of 70 monks. The *Skete* of the Prophet Elijah, half an hour away from the parent monastery on the verdant slopes, was once a *kelli,* or small monastic farm, but was granted to Paisij Welitschowskij, a charismatic Ukrainian reformer, in 1757. His influence drew Moldavian and Ukrainian followers to the *kelli,* which evolved into a *skete,* or loosely structured monastic community, where huts and dwellings radiate out from a central church. The *Skete* of the Prophet Elïjah was the first coenobitic house on Mount Athos, and the burgeoning numbers of Russian monks here moved the Patriarch, in the late nineteenth century, to limit Prophet Elijah's growth. With its history of iconoclasm, it is no surprise that the monks here boycotted the Patriarch's recent visit to the Holy Mountain. In protest against his ecumenicism, they shut themselves up in their church and cells and refused to greet the head of the Eastern Orthodox Church.

'Why are you smiling, Father?' I asked. 'How can I keep from smiling? I am happy, my child. Each day, each hour, I hear the mule's hoofbeats: I hear death approaching.'
NIKOS KAZANTZAKIS

In the vegetable garden of the Monastery of Pantokrator, a young, lithe ascetic tends the tomato vines. Whatever the monks have is freely given to visitors who need sustenance for the long treks between the monastic houses. On the Holy Mountain, food moves from hand to hand to hand. What is not used by the monasteries is passed on to isolated hermits in their huts and caves, which dot the rugged landscape. These are men who have abandoned all human fellowship to approach God; lone spiritual warriors who pay no heed to shelter, warmth or sustenance. They have faith that God, or their brothers, will provide.

'Thought I to myself, this is a real, genuine, unsophisticated live hermit; he is not stuffed like the hermit at Vauxhall, nor made up of beard and blankets like those on stage; he is a genuine specimen of an almost extinct race. What would not Walter Scott have given for him?'
THE HONORABLE ROBERT CURZON

On a cliff 30 metres (90 feet) above the sea, stands the Monastery of the Pantokrator, on the storm-lashed northeast coast of the Athonite peninsula. The easiest access, in good weather, is via caïque, the preferred mode of travel for monks making their way among the monasteries. Pantokrator was founded in the fourteenth century by the Byzantine commander Alexios, who liberated the island of Thassos from Turkish pirates, and his brother Ioannes. The monastery was subsequently granted aid by Emperor Ioannes V Palaeologos himself. During the Turkish occupation, when brutal taxes were levied on the monasteries, such benefactors as Catherine II of Russia came to Pantokrator's assistance. But periodic fires, most recently in 1948, have proven a more insidious foe than the Ottomans. Enclosed by an irregular polygonal wall, the monastery's buildings crowd a narrow interior courtyard. Immediately after the completion of the *Katholikon* in the fourteenth century, Pantokrator was decorated with fine murals executed in the Post-Panselenos Macedonian style. Today, both the old and the newer frescoes, restored by Matthaios Ioannou of Naoussa in 1854, survive. The wonder-working icon called the *Gerontissa,* or 'Elder', housed here, depicts the Virgin Mary, full length, standing alone. Legend has it that this icon once prompted a celebrant priest to hurry along with his recitation of the Liturgy. A venerable monk in the congregation was dying, and the Virgin intended him to take communion before he finally left this world for the next.

On Mount Athos, the monks keep alive the ancient Greek virtue of *philoxenia*, or hospitality to strangers. They see themselves as conduits for the love of God, and the classic Athonite greeting is 'Give me your blessing,' followed by the automatic response, 'It is the Lord's blessing.' More tangibly, visitors, pilgrims and summer labourers are offered lodging, food and refreshment.

Traditionally, upon arrival, guests are served *tsipouro*, a form of *ouzo*, *loukoumi*, or Turkish Delight, Greek coffee and cool water, some of the purest in Greece. Here, the *arhondaris*, or guest master, of Pantokrator serves *moustoukoulara*, biscuits made from grape must.

Though Athonite monks have many duties, they never allow their tasks—even the pleasant task of tending to devout visitors—to distract them from their primary activity, which is prayer. Mental prayer, or *karthiaki prosefhi*, 'prayer of the heart', is the monk's means of approaching God. Described by Nikephoros the Solitary, one of Mount Athos's greatest ascetics, the 'Jesus Prayer' is the key to opening a monk's heart to God. A simple prayer, it is repeated endlessly by Christians in monasteries all over the Orthodox world: 'Lord Jesus Christ, Son of God, have mercy upon me.'

During meals, one of the monks at an Athonite monastery reads aloud from a holy book, aware that the soul must be nourished even here in the refectory. All talking is thus eliminated, and even eating is raised to 'the spiritual plane'. St Ephraim the Syrian wrote:

'When the body is hungry and demands food, then remember that the soul, too, asks for its own proper food. And just as the body cannot live if it does not receive bread, so also the soul is dead if it is not nourished by means of spiritual wisdom. For man is dual, made up of soul and body, and this is why the Saviour said that man shall not live by bread alone.'

THE PELOPONNESE

TO ALL INTENTS AND PURPOSES, THE PELOPONNESE IS AN island, and an island-microcosm of everything most Greek. The country is cinched tight at the narrow Isthmus of Corinth and has been sliced in two, since 1893, by the Corinth Canal. Beneath the Corinthian Gulf, which severs it from mainland Greece, and washed on the east, west and south by the Aegean, Ionian and Cretan Seas, the Peloponnese, or 'Island of Pelops', billows out like a ragged dirndl skirt—spangled with fertile valleys, patterned with sun-bleached mountains and scalloped with sandy bays.

Islands, both inhabited and deserted, fringe the seemingly endless coastline. To the east lie the Argo-Saronic islands: Aegina, tiny Angistri, Poros, Hydra and Spetses. Off the extreme southern tip of the Peloponnese, lies Kythera, the birthplace of Aphrodite. To the west, below Patras, is Zakynthos, southernmost of the Ionian islands. In between, the 21,439 square kilometres (8,277 square miles) of the Peloponnese are as densely packed with historically, archaeologically and anthropologically significant sites as the books of Homer are with epithets. Greek history, from the Bronze Age, followed by the Roman, Byzantine and Frankish eras, down through the opening salvos of the War of Independence (1821), the Axis Occupation and the fiercely-fought Greek Civil War, has been written in Peloponnesian blood on Peloponnesian soil.

The Peloponnese is the true heartland of Greece, and the names on the modern map recall the events, heroes and drama of three millennia. Here, at Mycenae, was the seat of the warlike, Bronze-Age empire which eclipsed that of peaceful, Minoan Crete. Here, beneath steep, forbidding Mt Taïyetos, at Sparta, was the capital of Athens' dour, traditional rival among the Greek city-states. Here, the Doric temples to Apollo at Corinth and to Zeus at Olympia, illustrate the glory of Archaic Art, while at Bassae, near the present-day town of Andritsaina, the graceful Temple to Apollo *Epikourios,* 'The Helper', shelters beneath a state-of-the-art, 1,150 square-metre (1,375-square-yard) tent.

Cheek-by-jowl with these eloquent, classical marbles, the Peloponnese bristles with an imposing array of Stone-Age Greek, Roman, Byzantine, Crusader and Venetian castles. Many are complex conglomerates of fortifications erected over the course of all these martial eras, when the peaks and ridges of the peninsula served as refuges, watch towers and advance guard posts to protect against one invading force after another. The ancient citadel of Lerna, the work of Neolithic Peloponnesians, is some six thousand years old. Monemvasia, the 'Greek Gibraltar', was begun by the Byzantines in the sixth century and augmented by the Venetians in the fifteenth. Mycenae's fortress-acropolis boasts impressive and ponderous 'Cyclopean' walls—so called, because the Greeks believed such fortifications must have been the work of ancient giants, rather than mere mortals. Methoni, on the west coast of the prefecture of Messinia, was one of the strongest fortresses in all of Greece, even holding out against assault by the Athenians during the Peloponnesian War, and later becoming a pirates' lair before falling, at last, to Venice. The mountainous skyline and sheltered, natural harbours of the peninsula are dominated and fortified by these crenellated, once impregnable defences. Conquerors of every age have found the fertile Peloponnese, where spring arrives early and temperate valleys have long yielded bountiful crops, well worth fighting for.

But if the Peloponnese is seen today as quintessentially Greek, the same may not be said of the Peloponnesians. The history of southern Greece, the decimation of the entire population here in the eighth century, and the systematic repopulation with immigrant Slavs, points up the problem all Greeks have in establishing their identity.

Already settled in prehistoric times (3,000 BC), by people Herodotus called the Pelasgians, the first Peloponnesians to be called 'Greeks' on the peninsula were Indo-European tribes, Achaeo-Aeolians and Ionians, who emigrated from the Anatolian plains in about 2,000 BC. These early settlers, also known as the Achaeans, rapidly adapted, becoming far-ranging seamen, and making contact with the Minoans, whose civilization had spread throughout the southern Cyclades from Crete. Achaean culture, incorporating elements of the Cretan-Minoan, evolved into the civilization we know as the Mycenaean, whose sovereignty, by 1,300 BC, extended to Crete, the Aegean islands, the coasts of Asia Minor and Egypt, and to Cyprus, in addition to the Peloponnese.

This was the Bronze-Age culture immortalized by Homer in his *Iliad* and *Odyssey*. The poems, and their catalogue of men and ships dispatched to the Trojan War, reflect the very real glory that was Mycenae; a glory eclipsed in the twelfth century BC, when Dorian tribes swept down from the north, occupying Argolida, Corinthia, Lakonia and Messinia, ushering in the Greek 'Dark Ages'. The great Mycenaean fortress-cities were razed and burned and, for three centuries, Peloponnesian civilization was extinguished. In the eighth century, the population of the region had also been decimated by plague, which first broke out at Monemvasia. Repopulation of the entire region with Slavs occurred during the reign of Byzantine Emperor Constantine V. Christianized and rapidly assimilated, these new settlers changed the face of the Peloponnese, leading the German historian Fallmeyer, now largely discredited, to assert that the

Peloponnese had been peopled entirely by Slavs. In fact, the matter of the Modern Greeks' origins is still hotly disputed by scholars. Many linguists are attempting to substantiate either the Greeks' claim to be Greek, or the Slavs' claim that the Greeks are Slav, on the basis of place names and dialects. The matter is not yet settled.

What is not open to dispute, however, is that, following repopulation, the area was no longer sealed to the outside world of conquest and subjugation, a fact borne out by its subsequent seizure by the Franks, the Turks, the Palaeologue despots and the Venetians.

Throughout the following centuries of treacherous and violent 'foreign intervention', it would be the thorny, independent Maniotes, fortified in their characteristic, two- and three-storey tower-dwellings far to the south, who would symbolize the Peloponnesian resistance. Though the Ottomans and Venetians took the peninsula in turn; first one then the other seizing control, the Maniotes never accepted defeat. Just prior to the outbreak of the Greek War of Independence, the Peloponnese was in Turkish hands, administered from Tripolis: the Mani, however, had been a sovereign state within a state for six years, governed by the indomitable Petrobey Mavromichalis.

Foreign funding and allied military intervention determined the course of Modern Greek history. The Battle of Navarino, fought on 20 October 1827 by the allied fleets of England, France and Russia, off the western Peloponnesian coast near Pylos, signalled the beginning of the end for the Ottoman and Egyptian forces. In 1830, the Peloponnese was liberated. In 1831, the first President of Greece, Ioannis Kapodistrias, elected for a seven-year term, was assassinated by the brother and son of Petrobey Mavromichalis, and a fierce civil war followed on the heels of hard-won Greek independence.

Throughout the Peloponnese, a feeling of divisiveness brought on by the tenacity of centuries-old feuds and the maintenance of extremely localized traditions and customs, persists—the most indelible inheritance from a land split up since the fifth century BC into 'city-states' which fiercely guarded their sovereignty, their independence and their inalienable rights, as Spartans, Maniotes, Corinthians and Nafpliotes—but never as 'Greeks'.

In the abandoned structures of the depopulated Achaean mountain villages, and in the seige-tower-dwellings of such towns in The Mani as Vathia—bought up and preserved today by the Greek National Tourist Organization as expensive hostelries—the original inhabitants no longer live. But their conservative, suspicious and inward-looking world view, its windowless walls turned out in fear of the *xenos*, the 'foreigner' beyond the pale remains, immortalized in stone. The Peloponnese, in its entirety, is truly an island fortress, dominated by the high massif of the Taïyetos, studded with peaks defended since Neolithic times, and sheltering still a tenacious culture—Greek, and yet not-Greek—behind inviolable, 'Cyclopean' walls.

OPPOSITE TOP AND BOTTOM On the south coast of the Peloponnese, a great rocky trident of land stretches into the Sea of Crete. Here lies the inhospitable region known as the 'Deep Mani'. Nominally part of the prefecture of Lakonia, it is really another country, with its own customs, architecture and code of honour. This barren, rock-strewn and depopulated region is home to men whose pursuits, throughout history, were 'neither agricultural nor peaceful'. In such fortified towns as Kitta and Flomochori, their characteristic, Maniot tower-dwellings silhouetted against the clear, Peloponnesian sky, it is easy to see why the Maniotes are considered the true heirs of the bellicose ancient Spartans, known as the Lacedaemonians.

RIGHT The Deep Mani contains a treasure trove of eleventh- to fourteenth-century Byzantine churches, though the region resisted converting to Christianity until some four hundred years after St Patrick had Christianized Ireland. The tiny, roadside Church of the Panagheia, just outside the Maniot village of Nomitsi, is a humble representative of these small, sophisticated churches, many of which feature stunning frescoes, fine cloisonné masonry, intricately carved stone- and woodwork, and other elegant architectural features, rough exteriors belying rich interiors.

'Mani's history is a loose thread, interweaving itself with the multi-coloured strands from Sparta, Rome and Byzantium, the Franks, Venetians and Turks, but always creating a unique design of its own on the fringe of the main Greek pattern. It is a land of caves, churches and strange towers, of fortified villages on bare mountainsides, of Byzantine art and architecture of an extraordinary richness and importance, of feuds, fasting and lamentation. Until the present century it was almost a living fossil of the Middle Ages. It was a region of institutionalized civil war and chronic internal disorder, yet its ironic glory was to start the Revolution of 1821 which created the nation-state in which Mani itself became an incongruity. Today the towers are mostly deserted... Byzantine churches of great beauty, often magnificently frescoed, are collapsing through neglect... But though the visible pattern of Mani's long history is becoming sadly frayed, what remains is still fascinatingly intricate and woven on a fabric of coasts and mountains whose natural beauty can never be destroyed.'

PETER GREENHALGH AND EDWARD ELIOPOULOS

'O Turkish men, have you no shame
To war with womenfolk?
We are alone, our men are gone
To fight at Almiro.
But we with sickles in our hands
Will lop your heads like corn!'

MANIOT SONG

Near the village of Nomitsi, Maniot women, clothed in widows' weeds—for all have lost a father, husband or son—toil in the hot, Mediterranean sun. Wide-brimmed straw hats, characteristic of the region and made to order, afford some protection, but faces and hands are ravaged early due to prolonged exposure to the sun: the woman at the well is in her early 50s. Traditionally, Maniot women are as formidable as their men, and it was the women at work in the fields near Areopolis who defeated the 1,500 troops of Ibrahim Pasha in 1826. The Maniot men, greatly outnumbered, had concentrated their forces at Verga, in Messenian Mani, leaving their homes in the Deep Mani all but unprotected. Landing in Diros Bay, the Egyptians expected to encounter no resistance. But three hundred Maniot women, harvesting the crops and armed only with their scythes, their numbers augmented by an equal number of men who rushed in from outlying villages to aid in the defence, routed the superior Egyptian forces, driving them into the sea two days later. Areopolis was saved, and the myth of the Maniot Amazon was born into history.

OPPOSITE AND ABOVE 'Gytheion, to which a small island was tethered by a long narrow mole, trembled towards us through the afternoon haze. It was sunk in afternoon catalepsy. Nothing moved among the shipping and the cranes along the waterfront or among the inert tiers of houses that climbed the hill-side. Beyond the ship's awning the sun beat down like a curse and I could feel the heat of the quay through the soles of my shoes as though I were treading across a flat-iron. Every shutter was down. "Not a cat stirring," a fellow passenger said as we crossed the Sahara-like waterfront. "The only people about at such a time would be adulterers heading for an afternoon assignation. But perhaps not in Gytheion. It's not Athens, after all!…"…I woke up a couple of hours later. Sounds coming through the closed shutters indicated that the spell-bound town outside was stirring into life. Two rogue-wirelesses were in full blast and very strange they seemed after the unpolluted Mani. There was the exhaust of a motor or two, voices, a ship's siren, the clip-clop of horses and donkeys and the occasional clash of those portable brass scales that fruit-sellers and grocers hold up like statues representing Justice.'

PATRICK LEIGH FERMOR

'The fringes of the Greek world are dotted with enormous Venetian bastilles, each one a vast brooding complex of slanting curtain walls, miles of moat, donjons, flèches, demilunes, glacis, bastions, barbicans, redoubts, counterscarps, sally-ports and draw-bridges, all of well-nigh impregnable thickness. Slabs bearing the Lion and Latin inscriptions adorn them, commemorating some governor or general or gonfalionier called Zorzi, Mocenigo, Morosini or Bragadino.'

PATRICK LEIGH FERMOR

In Messenian Mani, on the westernmost 'tine' of the southern, Peloponnesian 'trident', Mt Aghios Nikolaos of Pylia terminates in a rocky promontory, washed on three sides by the Ionian Sea. Here stands the Venetian fortress known to the Europeans as 'Modon', and to the Greeks as Methoni. On the site of an ancient town once offered by King Agamemnon to Achilles, as long as the hero agreed to marry the king's eldest daughter, this defended harbour remained impregnable throughout the Bronze Age, up until the Peloponnesian War, falling only during the Roman occupation of Greece due to treachery on the part of Illyrian pirates, who disguised themselves as peaceful merchants to gain entry. Notorious as a pirates' lair in its own right, Methoni became a menace to Venetian shipping. The great Sea Republic sacked the city in AD 1125, and demolished its fortifications. Methoni remained in ruins during the Fourth Crusade, and was the first mainland Greek city to fall to the Franks. Subsequently refortified by the Venetians, who were well aware of its strategic value, the port was used as a stop-off on their long Mediterranean voyages. The last port in the Ionian became the largest fortress in the Peloponnese. A wide moat filled with sea water afforded additional protection, and on the tiny reef islet beyond the walls, the Venetians erected a tall, polygonal tower, which is still intact and mightily impressive to this day. The monumental main gate, opening onto the harbour, was completed in 1700, and reflects a change from the rough workmanship employed in the construction of the adjacent walls and towers.

ABOVE AND OPPOSITE In the northwestern prefecture of Eleia, the mountain town of Andritsaina is today visited primarily by visitors on their way to the nearby Temple of Apollo at Bassae. This traditional hill village, a market town with a population of 2,000, services some hundred smaller, surrounding hamlets and today seems like a throwback to the last century. Until recently, access was difficult. The town, precipitously situated on forested mountain slopes, is now reached via a good road, but Bassae, where the temple is obscured by protective canvas, is not a prime tourist destination and, as a result, Andritsaina has escaped extensive modernization. Here, on Sophocles Street, the tinsmith, greengrocer and the *pantopoleion*—or seller of everything—conduct business much as their forebears did a hundred years ago. The only concessions to the twentieth century are black and red olive containers, now made of plastic, and imported bananas. In fact, however, Andritsaina is home to a unique and priceless treasure: one of Greece's most valuable and extensive 'private' libraries. Donated by the son of Hatzi-Georgakis Nikolopoulos, a native of Andritsaina who emigrated to Smyrna in the eighteenth century, the library is now housed in an old, multi-storey school building on the outskirts of the town. The young scholar, born in 1786 and baptized Constantine, adopted the pseudonym 'Agathophron', or 'one of great virtue', early in life. Educated in Smyrna and Bucharest, he became an accomplished linguist, poet, author and composer, eventually moving to Paris, where he served as an assistant librarian at the Institute of France Library. His life's ambition, however, was to amass a library for his father's native Andritsaina, and to this end he impoverished himself. After 30 years of scrimping to buy the precious books, Agathophron summoned the mayor of Andritsaina and another townsman who would later become Prime Minister of Greece, and handed over 6,250 volumes which were transported by sea and mule to the Peloponnese.

'Years ago he had a lot of work. He made all kinds of tin boxes and cans, in many sizes for olive oil, sweets and paints. He sold buckets, dust-pans and water-cans, funnels, strainers, measures for wine and oil, all sizes of coffee pots for Greek coffee, feeding troughs for rabbits and churns, lanterns and oil lamps. He remembers making over a thousand lanterns a year when [there was] no electricity and at twilight housewives went about the house lighting one in every room. He also made small water canisters to hang over the sink when homes had no running water. He was also a tinker and asked to do repairs: he welded... patched... fixed...'

HELEN-FAY STAMATI

'...with all that's going on around me, all these new houses springing up, and old ones being restored, I can't help feeling a kind of sadness that my time is through and I'm no longer young, that I no longer have the strength to build just one more house . . . with walls almost a metre thick, each stone chiselled with my own two hands, each corner-stone carved by my best stone cutter. I wouldn't have partitions made with bricks like those they have today. Instead I would cut fine slender twigs to weave them in and out of wooden planks two inches wide nailed upright to the floor, same as my old master did so long ago. And I would spread the walls with plaster made with good sifted soil and bits of straw not with the trowel but with the palms of my hands.'

MASTER BUILDER GEORGIOS TSITSANIS

The two-storey dwellings lining Andritsaina's narrow, cobbled streets are, for the most part, traditional Peloponnesian houses, or *anokatogoi,* dating from the last century. A low-ceilinged ground floor, or *katoi,* traditionally supported a high-ceilinged *anoi,* or upper storey. The *katoi* was used for the storage of possessions, foodstuffs and staple goods, as well as for the shelter of domestic animals. The *anoi,* consisting of one or two partitioned rooms, was the principle dwelling area of the family. The house was entered, via the upper storey, from an exterior staircase which, before 1820, was usually removable and made of wood. The *katoi* in these market town buildings are used for shop space as well as storage. The streets of Andritsaina's central market, overhung by the *hagiati* balconies which bend in earth tremors but do not collapse, ring with the cries of merchants. The local *Agrofilakas,* or gendarme, discusses politics with a fellow townsman, gesticulating in the time-honoured Greek fashion to emphasize a point, as the butcher and greengrocers look on.

Monemvasia, a name which derives from *moni emvasis,* the Greek for 'single entrance', is a truncated mass of rock attached, tentatively, to the eastern coast of Lakonia by a slender modern causeway. A true island through the seventeenth century, and known as the 'Gibraltar of Greece', Monemvasia was settled in the sixth century AD by Lacedaemonians fleeing Sparta. Nearly 15 centuries of continuous habitation have made the now-depopulated town at the foot of the rock, and the Byzantine citadel-town, totally deserted atop the cliffs, a fascinating and unique architectural gem. Monemvasia's medieval heritage has been preserved and restored under the careful and informed guidance of two Athenian architects. Since 1964, both upper and lower towns have been under the aegis of the Greek Archaeological Service. The upper citadel has become an archaeological site, where no further building may take place, and the lower town, a historic monument, whose structures may be renovated only according to state-approved plans. Alexander and Haris Kalligas, the husband-and-wife team responsible for restoring the medieval buildings to their former glory, treat each commission with the same respect as an archaeological excavation – though they do not want the town merely preserved but lived in.

Drinking the Sun of Corinth

*Drinking the sun of Corinth,
reading the marble ruins, striding
vineyards and seas, sighting along
the harpoon a votive fish that slips
away, I found the leaves which the
sun's psalm memorizes, the living
land that passion joys in opening.*

*I drink water, cut fruit, thrust my
hand into the wind's foliage;
lemon-trees water the summer
pollen, green birds break my
dreams, I leave with a glance, a
wide glance, where the world
becomes again beautiful from the
beginning to the heart's measure.*
ODYSSEUS ELYTIS
(TRANS. KIMON FRIAR)

*Ornamental gourds for sale at a
road-side stand near Corinth, hay
drying on ropes strung in olive
trees, and grapes, ready for the
harvest, ripened in the
Peloponnesian sun, reflect the
country's continuing reliance on
agriculture, the abiding closeness
of the Greek to the soil.*

Our Land

We went up the hill to view our land—
shabby, scant fields, stones, olive trees.
Vineyards stretch down to the sea. A little fire
is smoking near the plough. With grandpa's clothes
we've made scarecrows for the jackdaws. Our days set out
in search of a little bread and much sunshine.
A straw hat glimmers under the poplar trees
The cock is on the fence. The cow is in the yellow.
How was it that we set our house and life in order
with a stone hand? On our door lintels
soot has gathered, year after year, from Easter candles—
tiny black crosses the dead have traced
on their return from the Resurrection. This land is much loved
with patience and with pride.
Every night from the dry well the statues come out cautiously and climb the trees.

YANNIS RITSOS
(TRANS. ANDONIS DECAVALLES)

Donkey saddles, or *samathia*, piled in Nea Figalia, tobacco in flower in Arkathiki and, later, drying under the olives: the cycle of the Greek year changes little off the modern highways and outside the built-up urban centres. Every city dweller has a village, and every villager his plot of earth, his olive trees, his wine press. At Easter, when the Greek returns *sto horio*, 'to the village', and Athens—*To Megalo Horio*, 'The Big Village'—empties, the essential, earth-stained nature of the Greek heart is revealed.

THE ISLANDS

THE IONIAN ISLANDS

NEAR THE END OF 1822, A YEAR AND A HALF AFTER THE bloody commencement of the Greek War of Independence, the statesman-scholar and future first historian of the new nation, Spyridon Trikoupis of Missolonghi, made a visit to the southernmost of the western Ionian islands. He was actually on his way to Corfu, or Kerkyra, summoned there by Frederick North, fifth Earl of Guilford, to assist in the founding of the Ionian Academy. But he made a detour to Zakynthos, or Zante, in order to visit the family of Dionysios Solomos, who were members of the displaced, Italo-Greek nobility. Like other Greeks of the Enlightenment, Trikoupis believed Greece's future lay as much in the hands of its educated classes, the literate few who could forge a national consciousness, as in those of the fierce *armatoles* and *klephts,* the rough chieftans who were busily tearing the Turks limb from limb.

Trikoupis, a close friend of Lord Byron, had come to Zante in search of a national poet, a 'Greek bard' who could offer a single cultivated voice to fire the imagination of cultivated Europe. His presence in the Ionians was no accident. Where else in long-enslaved Hellas was he more likely to find such a 'poet laureate' than on Corfu, Zante, Cephalonia or Ithaca, the islands which, for at least four centuries, had formed Greece's bridge with the thinkers of the 'civilized' West? Nurtured close against the mercenary hearts of Byzantium, Venice, France, Russia, and England, the Ionians had long been the Greek testing ground for all things 'Western', as well as a safe haven for all things most Greek: it was to the Ionians that Greece's best minds fled before the Turkish onslaught between the fourteenth and seventeenth centuries.

Dionysios Solomos, who embodied the answer to Trikoupis's quest, was born on Zakynthos in 1801, a natural son of Count Nicolas Salomon and a Greek serving-girl. He learned kitchen-Greek at his mother's knee, but was removed from her, and Zante, early on, to assume his rightful place as heir of the Doges and, ironically, of Dante and Byron, rather than Homer. Subsequently educated in Cremona and at the University of Padua, where he read law, Solomos's first poetry was composed in Italian but after tutoring in the Greek language from Trikoupis, the Ionians' most famous son, if not precisely 'native' son, began his

'If you are squeamish
Don't prod the beach rubble'
SAPPHO, TRANS. BY
MARY BARNARD

PREVIOUS PAGE At Porto Katsiki, 'Goat Port' beach, it is easy to see how the island of Lefkada, or Lefkas (the medieval Santa Maura) got its name. *Lefko* means white in Greek, and the white cliffs here drop 61 metres (200 feet) to the 'wine-dark' Ionian Sea on the southern tip of the island. South of the pearl-coloured sands at Porto Katsiki is the desolate spot known as Sappho's Leap. Where today there stands a modern lighthouse, there was once a famous Temple of Apollo from which a ritual leap, or dive into the sea was performed. The *katapontismos,* executed in the time of Strabo, released unrequited lovers from their misery, or served as some sort of trial. The victim-performers sometimes made the leap buoyed up by live birds; boats waited in the waves below to rescue survivors or collect victims. Sappho, the lyric poet of Lesvos, is said to have made the leap here, having despaired of achieving the love of one Phaon. More reliable accounts though have her dying at home in bed, attended by her daughter, Cleis.

Hymn to Liberty, the lyric poem in Demotic Greek that became the Greek national anthem, the Hellenic *Marseillaise.* Significantly, it was a passionate tirade against foreign oppression and intervention, and who better than an Ionian Greek to write about such matters?

Goethe called Solomos the 'Byron of the East', and the *Hymn* echoes Byron's *Don Juan* in its bitterness towards such masters of the *Eptanissa* (the 'Seven Isles', in Greek) as Great Britain. One of the great historical ironies of Modern Greece is that without oppression and foreign intervention and the resulting cultural education and enrichment that so characterizes the history of the Ionians, these islands would not have developed such a sophisticated society, so enlightened an aristocracy, nor such a body of Greeks passionately committed to liberty and democracy. Without the Venetians, the French and the English—who bound the Ionians in the fetters described so eloquently by Solomos—there would have been no Solomos at all. In fact, Greece's first poet laureate never set foot on the mainland. Though a fervent nationalist, Solomos's eyes and heart were trained, like a true Ionian's, on the West. The Ionians, so close, geographically speaking, to the benighted Balkans were, ideologically, seven European stepping stones to the East.

The 'Eptanissa' of today actually number more than 20 islands, at least 17 currently inhabited, but take their Greek name from the major members of the group: Corfu, the Paxi (Paxi and Andipaxi), Lefkada (or Lefkas), Ithaca, Zakynthos and Kythira. All but Kythira, the odd-island-out in terms of geography and modern history, lie in the Ionian Sea, between Italy and the Greek mainland. Corfu, the northernmost and most important island, hugs the coast of Albania, and is closest to Italy. The straits between Corfu and Albania have been vigilantly patrolled in recent years: tourists straying into Albanian waters risk being shot, as do political refugees swimming to seek asylum in Greece.

Beneath Corfu range small, densely cultivated Paxi and Andipaxi, green jewels taken over in summer by British tourists, and Lefkada, a peninsula until the seventh century BC, when a canal severed it from the mainland. Today, visitors reach Lefkada via a pontoon bridge. Ithaca, home to Odysseus in the Homeric epics, and today a left-wing stronghold, is farther south and nestles above Cephalonia, mountainous and depopulated, the largest of the Ionians, and Zakynthos, called by the Venetians the 'Flower of the Levant' and home to the endangered sea turtle *Caretta caretta.* It is a long, circuitous voyage from Zakynthos, which lies approximately 16 kilometres (10 miles) off the Peloponnesian coast, to Kythira, located some 290 kilometres (180 miles) to the southeast, around the Maniot trident.

Kythira, too, due to its geographical location, has not shared in the tourist boom experienced by its fellow Ionians to the west. Led by Corfu, one of the Mediterranean's choicest holiday destinations, the western Ionians' crystalline waters and ice-white sands have drawn visitors in droves since the 1960s. The last in the centuries-long list of conquerors, these North European friends have already succeeded in loving much of coastal Corfu to death. The beach communities, overrun in summer, have suffered, both ecologically and in the human sphere. No Greek at all is heard in some villages in season, and no Greek hospitality tendered. The tourists are seen by many Corfiotes and Cephalonians as modern marauders.

A history of the Ionians reads like a secular Book of Numbers, one heir begetting another in the islands' dense and murderous chronology. From the eighth century BC forward, when Corinth colonized Corfu, and on down through a succession of conquerors including the Macedonians, Sicilians, Epirotes and Romans; followed by the Byzantines, Normans, Venetians, Genoans, Neapolitans, Turks, French, Russians and, finally, the British, the Ionians have been considered a prize at any cost. In 1204, when the Fourth Crusade, under the Doge of Venice, took Constantinople, and the Eastern Empire was dismembered, Enrico Dandolo carved up the Ionians, serving them out among his trusted colleagues. The Italian presence was firmly entrenched on Corfu, the Paxi, Cephalonia, Ithaca and Zakynthos; Lefkada alone remained temporarily in Greek hands. Kythira, after 1207, and for centuries afterwards, remained a possession of the Veniero family. Won and lost, and won again by successive Doges, the Ionians would be, for the most part, islands of the Venetian lagoon up to and including the eighteenth century. The Turks posed the greatest threat in the region, but only Cephalonia would be an unwilling participant in the long, dark night of Turkish occupation. On other islands, a Venetian Gold Bull (Edict) protected the rights and privileges of the Greek Orthodox residents, vouchsafing their religious freedom and affording them a status unheard of in those parts of the country held by the Turks. Something else which afforded the Greek Orthodox inhabitants with greater security was the institution, and devaluation of the *Livro d'Oro*, enabling them to purchase titles as good as those held by their Catholic masters.

What centuries of conquest, both military and cultural, have not succeeded in destroying, however, is now threatened by tourism, and tourism of the sort no traditional culture can withstand. The dense waves of single-country package tourism, and the invasion, in summer, of the European underclass, with its dark legacy of drugs and crime, is undermining the solid structure of Greek life in the Ionians. Saddest of all is the plight of the loggerhead turtles of Zakynthos. These peaceful visitors to the sandy Ionian beaches have been returning to lay their eggs here each summer for millions of years, sharing the sea and sand with the Venetians, the Turks, and all other visitors to the area, only to succumb, in the late twentieth century, to tourists' tent poles, dune buggies, amplifiers, electric lights and garbage. The timely education of residents and tourists alike, and conservation practised by such charitable organizations as the Greek Sea Turtle Protection Society and the work of Goulandris Museum of Natural History may be too late to preserve the life and liberty of these unsung and silent Zakynthians for the next millennium.

'After dinner I hear the low whistle of the man by the sea and I go out on to the balcony. He is shipping his baskets and tridents and screwing his carbide-lamp to the prow. Tonight I am to try my hand at this peculiar mode of fishing. The tridents are four in number and varying in size; besides them we ship the octopus hook—attached to a staff about the size of a billiard cue—for octopus is not stabbed direct but coaxed: whereas squid and fish are victims of a direct attack… The night is deep and clean-smelling and utterly silent. Far out under the Albanian hills glow the little flares of other carbide-fishers. Anastasius circles in the margin of rocks below the house and begins to talk quietly, explaining his practice. Midges begin to fly into our faces and we draw down our sleeves to cover our arms. He rows standing up and turning his oars without breaking the surface—since it is into this spotless mirror that we must gaze, and the least motion of wind smears all vision. Presently the carbide lamp is lit and the whole miraculous underworld of the lagoon bursts into a hollow bloom—it is like the soft beautiful incandescence of a gas-mantle lighting. Transformed, like figures in a miracle, we gaze down upon a sea-floor drifting with its canyons and forests and families in the faint undertow of the sea—like a just-breathing heart.'
LAWRENCE DURRELL, 1960

In the little working fishing harbour of Lygia, on the northeast coast of Lefkada, caïques with butane gas-lamps, called *pyrofania* in Greek ('fire crowns'), are ready for the night's work. Used for squid- and octopus-fishing, the boats will ply the waters between the mainland and the island, bringing back a catch which will be sold to the tourist restaurants on the quay.

'A young woman and her mother invested many years of labour in producing the items that covered all the interior surfaces of the house. Since they were usually the only items of value in the house, they were highly visible.'
'Whereas women once were the creators, provisioners, and guardians of the interiors of their houses, they are now only the caretakers.'
ELEFTHERIOS PAVLIDES/JANA HESSER

ABOVE AND OPPOSITE In Lefkas Town, Eva Yannopoulou has transformed a private home into a stunning folk museum. Her daughter, Donna, who here wears the traditional costume of an Ionian island bride, may work in the busy tourist trade by day, but she has learned the traditional art of fine needlework at home. In the past, a girl would have to learn to sew so that she could marry. As characteristic as the *boustina*, or

white bodice, ornamented with gold and jewels, the *peseli* or *kremezo*, the gold-trimmed jacket, that make up her costume, are the meticulously worked cushion covers and wall hangings in the *saloni*, or sitting room. Many examples of Lefkada's elaborately patterned needlework are displayed today at the Benaki Museum in Athens, part of the treasured national heritage created by Greek women.

'To plant a new vineyard, the earth must first be ploughed and hollows made at intervals of one metre, in which vine cuttings are planted. To ensure a good harvest, the vines must be rigorously pruned and the dry twigs removed. The earth around the roots is dug with a mattock and then hoed to destroy the weeds. Incisions are made in the branches to produce larger grapes and the vines are sprayed against disease. Grapes to be dried as raisins are harvested at the end of July. The grapes are picked and spread to dry. They are shuffled with a pitch-fork and leaves and twigs are removed with a rake. To remove the stalks and rotten raisins they are winnowed by hand and then tossed in a bucket-like colander to remove dirt and grit. At the time of the vintage a guard keeps watch over the vineyards from a thatched hut set in a tree or on stilts. The vintage begins with much celebrating in the middle of September, after the feast of the Holy Cross. Bunches of grapes are cut from the vine with a small knife and piled up beside the vineyard. Certain types of grapes are selected for eating while others are pressed to extract the juice. The grapes are then put in a wooden or basket-sided vat and trodden by one or several people. A wooden club may also be used to pound them. In recent times large stone vats have been built next to the vineyards. They adjoin underground cisterns where the must is stored.'

NIKI PSARRAKI-BELESIOTI

Outside Lefkas Town, workers in the vineyards take part in the annual grape harvest.

from *The Sacred Way*

And then! as they came near to
where I sat
the Gypsy saw me—before I had
seen him well—,
drew the tambourine from off his
shoulder,
beat upon it, and with his other
hand
tugged the chain with force. And
the two bears
rose on their hind-legs heavily.
The one,
the larger (she was the mother
certainly),
her head adorned with tassles of
blue beads,
with a white amulet on top, rose
up
suddenly enormous, as if she were
the Great Goddess's primordial
image,
the Eternal Mother's, she who
divinely sad,
as with time she assumed a human
form,
was in her longing for her daughter
called
here Demeter, in her longing for
her son
elsewhere Alcmeme or the
Madonna.
And the small bear beside her, like
a big
toy, like an innocent child, rose up
as well
submissive, not guessing yet its
suffering's length
nor the bitterness of slavery
mirrored in
the burning eyes the mother turned
upon him.
ANGHELOS SIKELIANOS, TRANS. BY
EDMUND KEELEY AND PHILIP SHERRARD

A Lefkada woman crochets while
watching her sheep; another tends
to her herbs and vegetables in a
well-watered garden; and a gypsy,
part of a community welcomed in
the Ionians in the fifteenth century
for their skill in horse-breeding,
parades his dancing bear in the
streets of Lefkas Town.

THE AEGEAN ISLANDS

FOR THE GREEK, AS FOR THE FOREIGN VISITOR, THE AEGEAN islands conjure up images of summer, sandy beaches, simplicity and, most vividly, of the sea. Thrown like vulnerable, bright dice into the dark water these islands, and their Greek inhabitants, have always depended upon the sea: what it brought to their shores, and what it took away.

In the words of the Byzantines, the sea was *synappei mallon i temnei,* 'uniting, rather than dividing'. It was the medium all islanders knew best, and the medium they were driven to dominate. Communication was as important as commerce to these seamen. Only on rare occasions in the islands' long and convoluted history, have the disparate, isolated communities allowed themselves to be cut off, from one another, and from the world. Though at first the sea brought primarily obsidian blades, metals, pottery, and foodstuffs from neighbouring isles, eventually whole, alien worlds crowded past the islanders' doors, with all the surprises and risks involved in such invasions. The history of the Greek relationship with the sea is at least nine thousand years old, and though the vessels in the Aegean have changed dramatically over the millennia, the crewmen have remained much the same.

The first representations of Greek seamen and the Aegean sea are carved on Cycladic cult objects dating from the 3rd millennium BC, though the islanders' first attempts at navigation had begun some four millennia earlier. The great Minoan thalassocracy (from the Greek for 'sea', *thalassa*) rose in the 2nd millennium BC. Palatial Knossos had its sea cults, and its Priestess of the Winds, part of the wind cult mentioned in the *Iliad.* Cycladic sailors, too, turned to the goddesses for favourable winds: both the names of their Amphitrite and Aphrodite trailed such epithets as 'fair sailing', 'sea-borne', 'harbouring' and 'leader of ships'.

With the decline of the Minoans on Crete, mastery of the seas passed to the Mycenaeans, Jason's quest for the fleece and the conflict at Troy reflecting the concerns and character of Greece's second great maritime empire. Bronze-Age kings contributed 1,186 ships to the Trojan campaign, many hailing from home ports in the Aegean. During this period of military might, such works of art as Santorini's great Fresco of the Fleet (1550–1500 BC), painted on the walls at

Akrotiri, reflect an Aegean world not only materially enriched by maritime commerce and conquest, but culturally sophisticated as well.

Mycenae fell before the advance of the Dorians, who subsequently invaded the Cyclades, the Dodecanese and Crete. During the Greek Dark Ages, the islanders' world closed down around them for three centuries, and seamanship was limited to fishing; sea travel confined to brief visits to neighbouring islands and more distant voyages never attempted.

Today's visitors to the Aegean are surprised at the cultural diversity displayed on these rocky outcrops in the sea. Islands as geographically close as Mykonos, Tinos and Syros are, in significant ways, as different as sovereign states. The reasons for the variety and richness of the customs, costumes and character of the Greek islands lie in their divergent histories, an island long a pirates' lair differing greatly from a neighbour that served as the seat of Catholic bishops.

The archipelago itself spills over some 644 kilometres (400 miles) of sea. The total number of Greek islands, some 2,000, may still be a matter of conjecture for cartographers, but only 50 or so are usually included on the tourist maps, and two have gone dark and nameless—on Greek maps, at least—off the Dardanelles. Formerly Greek Tenedos and Imvros were lost to Turkey in 1923, and only token Greek-speaking communities remain there now.

But though the islands bordering Turkey today serve as heavily militarized zones of readiness for the next Aegean conflict between Moslem and Christian, the other islands are booming centres of tourism. In fact, Greek culture in the region seems to thrive on adversity. There is some rare gift for endurance and triumph in a spirit that can face such devastating blows as the 1822 Massacre of Chios, when at least 25,000, some say 60,000, Chiotes were annihilated by the Turks under Kara Ali Pasha, the survivors enslaved or carried off to Turkish harems. Sixty years later, an earthquake decimated the island's population again, destroying most houses and public buildings. And it is a testament to tenacity and faith that despite the devastation, the Chiotes rallied. In 1912, the Greek army drove out the Turks and, today, Chios is a prosperous holiday destination and centre of the arts. Building on the rubble, again and again, is an Aegean *leitmotif.*

If the tune varies, the theme remains constant throughout the islands. History may have dictated a changing cast of masters, but the islanders' actual and existential position throughout the millennia has remained constant, unalterable: at the mercy of the sea, one becomes master of the sea. Whether Serifiote or Skyrian, the island seaman pounded his octopus and repaired his nets on the shore of the natural harbour, drawing his caïque up on the sand. But his loved ones lived at the top of the hill, beyond the skein of alleyways he and his brothers tangled on purpose to slow the feet of pirates, be they Cretan, Genoan or Slav. Today, just as in the thirteenth and fourteenth centuries, visitors lose their way in the *hores,* or 'main towns' of Mykonos, Skyros and Patmos, though they need no longer fear being doused with boiling oil poured down from the second storeys of the captains' houses – a deterrent to marauders in the past.

The labyrinthine island villages, despite the thousands of unwelcome visitors who have entered to pillage and been forced to inch their way along whitewashed walls in exceedingly narrow lanes, remain quintessentially Greek. Built on the bedrock of the Orthodox faith, they preserve within their walls an architectural philosophy and a traditional way of life which proceeds according to a relentless seasonal and ecclesiastical pattern, tested and tempered over grim centuries. The Aegean existence, looking, as it does, to nature in the form of the sea, the sun and the wind for direction, has withstood all efforts to erase it. Astoundingly, it is even withstanding the siren song of the twentieth century.

Most islanders today know that what they have guarded is of inestimable value, even if the returns are largely intangible. Though the weavers of Mykonos, with their unweildy looms, and most of Skyros's woodcarvers, Santorini's tinsmiths and carpenters, and many of Syros's confectioners are gone, their descendents now involved in the tourist industry, the crafts of a bygone era are being revived and fostered in co-ops in the islands, in Athens, and throughout Greece. What is no longer preserved in private homes—for example, the intricately layered Cycladic roof, with its strata of oak, chestnut, cane, seaweed, earth, mortar and lime—is painstakingly documented in texts and duplicated in folk museums.

Nor have the most heavily visited areas been allowed to degenerate. Even on Mykonos, inundated in high season by an army of visitors, Greek life goes on apace. As described by David Holden, it is 'the leaping spark of tension that is the only certain characteristic of Greekness. Spirit and flesh, ideal and reality, triumph and despair—you name them and the Greeks suffer or enjoy them as the constant poles of their being, swinging repeatedly from one to the other and back again, often contriving to embrace both poles simultaneously, but above all never reconciled, never contented, never still.'

This eternal dialectic, a dance on tip-toe between extremes—between East and West, Ottoman and Venetian, the sea and the land—is the essence of life in the Aegean. The islanders know the steps, treasure the dance, and the circle is unbroken, but for the kerchief connecting the second dancer in the chain of dancing islanders to the leader. Visitors may look on, and even learn the rudiments, but the island dance is performed, first and foremost, for the residents.

It is significant that Homer's hero, the wily Odysseus, who questions the blind seer, Tiresias, about his fate, is told that if it is a peaceful death he wants, he must walk inland, and find a place where the people neither know what an oar is, nor salt their food. Odysseus, like all island Greeks, would have found it impossible to imagine such a place, let alone seek it out: an island life may never have been peaceful but, for Odysseus and his heirs, any other has always been, and will continue to be, inconceivable.

ABOVE AND RIGHT Kambos, the fertile plain stretching along the island of Chios' east coast, is today one enormous orchard, its cisterns and donkey-powered water wheels graphic reminders of the days of Genoese rule. (In 1261, the Genoese were granted the permission of the Byzantine emperor to settle in Chios, according to the terms of the Treaty of Nymphaeum. In 1346, they laid seige to Kastro and occupied Chios by force).

Nea Moni, a monastery housing stunning frescoes, located among cypress trees west of the capital, was built in 1049 on the spot where the Virgin is said to have appeared to the faithful in a myrtle tree.

'On these high slopes the goats amble and graze. Their bells sound from far off. Their blacks and browns and whites fleck the grey rock. Ever preoccupied, their ignorance of time makes their motions peaceful to watch. One wonders why it is that the expression of their orange eyes should be so suspicious. The herdsmen seem as though in a trance of waiting. Drenched in sunlight they sit motionless or walk so unhurriedly it seems they scarcely move of their own volition. It is an existence wholly of daydream… Pan and the nymphs are the very essence of a shepherd's midday reveries… notes of the pipe are the music of those hourless, passive days.'

'As you come down the further side you begin to meet the people coming up to their high fields. Greetings are quietly exchanged; you are still under the quiet spell of the dawn which people instinctively hesitate to violate. Soon you enter the lanes in between fields and orchards and suddenly you see people at work picking fruit or hoeing in their gardens. Their clothes give them protective colouring so that they seem like the cicadas in the trees, only visible when one's vision is directed right upon them and rightly focused. And as you go on through mile upon mile of this wealth of fertility you marvel at the spilling cornucopia harvests…'
CHRISTOPHER KININMONTH

'We arrived in Chios in the evening and I went to sleep. At four o'clock in the morning I suddenly woke up. It seemed to me that some terrible animal, a large beast was trying to lift the house to get through. Its back was like the sea, swelling and falling. It was an earthquake. Lying in bed, which was rocking like a swing, I was waiting to see what would happen. I thought to myself: "Will the house come down? Are our days up or shall we still see the sun tomorrow?" The bed stopped moving and we suffered no harm. But, in all fairness, when the earthquake started I was worried. I did not feel at ease. The first swaying of the bed was somewhat unpleasant; the second one seemed more bearable to me; by the third one I was almost used to it. In fact, when it was all over I felt almost sorry. That earthquake has a philosophy of its own. All Greeks should come and spend one night in Chios. They will then come to understand what the fate of the Greeks is... They are not stable as yet and they perpetually move. They do not know today what will happen to them tomorrow and they think to themselves: "Will everything suddenly collapse or shall we enjoy the sun of life again in the morning?"'

YIANNIS PSYCHARIS, 1888

'The monk was sitting in his hermitage and was telling a story. Beside him Constantine, who had just arrived at Chios and destined to become emperor, was listening to the old man carefully: "While I was walking around with my companion one day," started the monk, "I saw light in a bush. I asked my friend to go and see what it was, but as soon as he went near, the light vanished. This went on for three days. On the fourth day we decided to set all the bushes on fire. Sure enough, we did this and everything was burnt except for a small myrtle bush. We then went near, had a close look and found an icon of the Virgin Mary lying under it. We brought the icon to our hermitage and went to sleep. The next morning when we woke up the icon had disappeared. We searched everywhere but couldn't find it. We then went to the myrtle bush and there it was, in exactly the same place where we had first found it. We took it back to the hermitage, but the following morning it had disappeared once again. We understood that the Virgin Mary wanted to be worshipped at exactly that spot, so we built the shrine that you now see. We placed the icon inside and it has never gone away since."'
JULIEN GALLAND

The cheesemaker, baker and packsaddler of Volissos, on Chios, practice their ancient arts, unchanged by this century's tastes and technologies.

'In rural Chios, time has virtually stood still, and many of the islanders live today very much as they did hundreds of years ago. Only the occasional television antenna perched atop a traditional ceramic-tiled roof, reveals that the residents have been touched, however lightly, by twentieth century technology. There are some 24 villages in central Chios devoted solely to the cultivation of the mastic tree, and their inhabitants, many wearing the traditional dress of their forefathers, still travel by donkey or mule every morning to tend the groves of trees that provide them with their livelihood. The cultivation of the mastic tree is difficult, and demands a great deal of attention. In the villages of Pyrgi, Kalimassia, Neo Hori, as well as the other 21 mastic-producing villages, the mastic trees are tended much as they have been for generations. The young trees are planted early in the spring, fertilized and purged of pests. Only after 15 years does the mastic tree begin to produce resin. However, the mastic farmers "embroider" the trees when they are only six years old; using a special tool, they make shallow incisions on the trunks and branches of the trees, from which the viscous mastic weeps and falls onto the ground. The mastic is allowed to lie upon the ground for 15 to 20 days to crystallize, at which time it is gathered by the villagers into wicker baskets.'
STEPHANIE GINGER AND
CHRISTOPHER KLINT

In medieval Pyrgi, on Chios, tomatoes hang to dry on a pistachio-green balcony. These present-day Chiotes have preserved the eleventh-century mastic town's characteristic architectural ornamentation, using the modern materials of concrete and brick in addition to the traditional plaster.

'Exterior surfaces are plastered only in the village of Lithi, and where repairs have taken place. In Pyrgi, however, and in a few isolated houses in other villages, the façades have decorative motifs executed on a plaster surface, known as xysta. This is an unusual decorative technique, perhaps unique in Greece, that produces a striking effect. The entire façade is divided into horizontal bands filled with black and white geometric shapes. The motifs are simple: triangles, rhombuses, circles, semicircles and herring bone patterns. The technique is based on the black sand in the plaster; this is carefully whitewashed and the design is scraped away (xysta means "scraped"), leaving the black motifs against a white ground. It is similar, in other words, to the technique of the Italian sgraffiti.'
CHARALAMBOS BOURAS

'The characteristic features of the northern villages are their poverty and the rudimentary planning. They are an example of a genuinely "folk" architecture…which was built of local materials, by the users of the houses themselves, employing the simplest methods. The material available for study is limited in extent, and decreases with each passing day, as in all the villages new dwellings replace the small houses that have no amenities. In the larger settlements at Volissos and Kardamyla, almost nothing is left of the traditional houses, which began to be replaced long ago…The structure of the houses in the northern villages is very simple. The masonry is of limestone rubble, and the binding agent is mud instead of lime-cement. Dressed corner-stones, in doorways or at the corners of walls, are rare. A few arches and vaults, reminiscent in form of those of Hora, or the mastic villages, are to be found in Kardamyla, Pityos and Volissos…The wooden structures are equally primitive. The stylos [wooden pillar supporting roof] is usually an unworked treetrunk, as is the main beam supporting the mesodoki [main beam in roof]…The roofing could equally well be described as pitched or flat. It is made of joists, sea-weed and myrtle branches, like the roofs of other Aegean villages, but it has a distinct slope…In an architecture as simple, poor and unpretentious as this, it is difficult to speak of architectural forms, since they all derive directly from the structure.'
CHARALAMBOS BOURAS

BELOW An enticing and highly decorative vaulted church interior in mastic-rich Pyrgi is a dramatic contrast to the crumbling farmhouses and simple, utilitarian façades of these two-storey houses found in the humble town of Volissos, located on the desolate northwest tip of Chios.

In Hora, Mykonos's main town, situated on the island's picture-postcard harbour, the area called Little Venice looks westward towards the summer sunset and the sacred isle of Delos. The cubistic, whitewashed captains' houses of the eighteenth and nineteenth centuries, with their royal blue and burnt sienna balconies, have today been converted into bars and tourist shops, the original architectural elements faithfully preserved or duplicated. The *kapasi,* or chimneys, whitewashed and incised with patterns, punctuate the rooftops, dwarfed by television antennae. With their elegant backs turned on the sea, these typical 'broad-fronted' Cycladic houses front onto a narrow alleyway which threads its way into Kastro, the oldest part of Hora. Kastro, one of two early fortified settlements on Mykonos, was a place of refuge from the sea raids to which Hora was subjected up until the middle of the seventeenth century. It is difficult for modern visitors, sipping their Campari, and watching a fisherman beating an octopus on the stones, to imagine the misery of life in the medieval 'fortress'. But the contemporary residents of crowded Hora, joined by seasonal visitors in their thousands, are just as grateful for the *Meltemi,* the powerful north wind, that makes summer in the streets of Kastro almost bearable.

'The white color of the houses, churches and even the seams between the flagstones in the street, constitutes the main unifying element in the Mykonian town plan. This, in combination with the intimacy given to the street by the ledges, the staircases, and the seats (as well as the use of the street and the generally human scale) gives the impression of an interior with a blue sky for a ceiling.'
ARISTEIDIS ROMANOS

'The first of May is celebrated throughout Greece as the festival of spring. The festivities commence at dusk on the eve of May Day by a general exodus to the gardens and fields for the purpose of making wreaths to welcome May. In the larger towns these wreaths are sold ready-made at the florist's; those who wish to be in keeping with tradition buy a wreath and nail it over their front door. However, flowers may be a poetic symbol of joy and spring for the inhabitant of the city, but for the farmer they are sterile and useless things. They cannot symbolize what he holds most dear: the earth's protection and favour for a good crop and an abundance of fruit. For this reason farmers do not use flowers… but various green plants and fruit…'

GEORGE A. MEGAS

Skyros, largest of the four Northern Sporades islands, is home to the famous, and endangered, Pikermic breed of small, half-wild horses. Whether these tiny ponies are descended from the Hipparion or the Tarpan, is a matter of debate, but they are remarkably similar to the steeds depicted in the Parthenon frieze. Many legends are associated with Skyros. Here, Theseus was killed by the king of Skyros, Lycomedes. Achilles was hidden on the island by his mother to prevent his enlistment to the Trojan War. Skyros Town, or Hora, the island capital, with its largely intact Byzantine and Venetian settlement of Kastro, seems to have been caught in a time warp as well. On the town's main street—the street of the *Megala Strata,* or Venetian-era aristocracy—Skyrian men sit in an all-male *kafeneion,* decked out in the baggy bloomers of the Turkish occupation, and the characteristic, laced, Skyrian shepherds' sandals, the *trohadia.* The interiors of Skyros's traditional houses are also a throwback to centuries past. On shelves which circle the whitewashed sitting rooms, priceless porcelain, faïence and crystal are proudly displayed. Beneath these more fragile heirlooms, hang copper plates, trays and pans.

Embroidered coverlets, cushion covers and runners complete the array of personal wealth on show, and Skyrian needlework designs are traditional and distinctive. Each Skyrian house is a kind of family museum for the parading of family wealth and skill. Skyros's religious festivals are also a display of wealth, in this case, cultural. Such events as the annual Goat-Dance of Skyros, a weird and wonderful costumed ritual enacted by Skyrian men on the steep streets of Hora, may be a Pagan legacy, Dionysian rites thinly Christianized. During this dance, which occurs during Greek *Apokries,* or Carnival, the men transform themselves into *Yeri,* or a sort of bogey-man. Disguised in kids'-skin masks, and harnessed in hundreds of pounds of shepherds' bells, they lurch and shake, creating an unholy racket up and down the narrow alleys. Skyros's ancient traditions and lore, as well as priceless artefacts, if not actually preserved in situ, are housed and documented in the excellent local Faltaïts Museum. Founded by the heir to one of the island's 'first families', the museum is located in the family's nineteenth-century mansion, itself just adjacent to the site of an ancient Skyrian temple that was dedicated to the goddess Astarte.

'On a rock, so utterly barren and hopeless of vegetation, that…I can scarcely discover, on its whole surface, one speck of verdure, rises in dazzling whiteness and beauty this singularly interesting city…The harbour, from the abrupt sides and bottom of which the town starts up theatrically, is neither spacious nor secure. It is, in fact, a deep bay, situated on the western side of the island, and still open to the west, having no nearer protection from that quarter than the opposite coast of the Morea, which may be four or five miles distant.'

GEORGE WADDINGTON,
1823—1825

Tiny, rocky Hydra, easily accessible today by hydrofoil from the port of Piraeus, is a member of the Argo-Saronic island group, along with Aegina, Spetses and Poros. Its exquisite harbour, and rising tiers of nineteenth-century mansions, all well preserved and maintained as summer homes by ship owners and wealthy Athenians, were built by the island's captains during Hydra's heyday in the late eighteenth and early nineteenth centuries. Protected under Greek law against tasteless development, Hydra is a traffic-free island, its polished flagstones open to two- and four-footed traffic alone. Donkeys, long abandoned elsewhere in Greece, are prevalent on Hydra, where they are used to transport building supplies, foodstuffs, and tourists to the monasteries located on Mount Klimakion.

LEFT AND FAR LEFT Hydra is now home to a cosmopolitan mix of artists and writers in high season, maintaining a reputation as an intellectuals' colony. Off season, few places can seem colder, when locals and rare visitors congregate in bars, restaurants, private homes and, more recently, video-cafés. Signs in the main town, on the harbour-side, inform donkey drivers against tethering their beasts—the warning is largely ignored; colourful, hand-painted placards advertise Ioannis Kokoris, fruiterer, and the butcher shop of Constantine Pavlos. Hydra has a thriving *agora* where produce fills a little town square.

'Our mate was a Hydriot, a native of that island rock which grows nothing but mariners and mariners' wives. His character seemed to be exactly that which is generally attributed to the Hydriot race; he was fierce, and gloomy, and lonely in his ways…It seemed to me that the personal freedom of these sailors, who own no superiors except those of their own choice, is as like as may be to that of their sea-faring ancestors. And even in their mode of navigation they have admitted no such an entire change as you would suppose probable; it is true that they have so far availed themselves of modern discoveries as to look to the compass instead of the stars, and that they have superseded the immortal gods of their forefathers by St Nicholas in his glass case, but they are not yet so confident either in their needle, or their saint, as to love an open sea, and they still hug their shores as fondly as the Argonauts of old…These seamen, like their forefathers, rely upon no winds unless they are right astern, or on the quarter; they rarely go on a wind if it blows at all fresh, and if the adverse breeze approaches to a gale, they at once fumigate St Nicholas, and put up the helm. The consequence of course is…they are blown about in the most whimsical manner.'
A. W. KINGLAKE

In the whitewashed village of Oia, located atop the precipitous, 305-metre (1,000-foot) high cliffs on the northern tip of Santorini (or Thera), mule-drivers congregate at the top of the serpentine, cliff-side road that connects Oia with its port below. Oia, largely levelled when an earthquake brought death and destruction to Santorini in 1956, has been rebuilt, income from tourism and shipping financing the mansions and hotel-complexes that now characterize this busy summer resort. Santorini, southernmost of the Cyclades, is only 113 kilometres (70 miles) north of Crete. Without doubt, it is the most dramatically beautiful spot in Greece, and the vast, sunken *caldera,* or bay, which filled with sea-water following the *c.* fifteenth-century BC eruption of the volcano here, compares with the Grand Canyon in majesty. In antiquity, the island was known as Strongyle (The Round One), and Kalliste (The Fairest), until the explosion that blew its centre sky-high: the blast would have made Krakatoa's eruption seem like the pop of a champagne cork by comparison. When the volcanic dust and ash settled, 'the round one' had been split asunder, forming a group of unsteady islets circling a hot lagoon. Today, the island is coping with a cataclysm of another sort: tourism. Building codes and strong local government have preserved the island's culture and distinctive, barrel-vaulted architecture, and village life seems largely unaffected by the influx of holidaymakers. In fact, visitors are cleverly 'quarantined' in certain designated areas, outside which traditional Greek life proceeds with its cycle of saints' day celebrations, its annual harvests of grapes, tiny Santorini tomatoes and chick peas, as well as the round of civic events.

'When the Venetians left Tinos in
1715, the Greek inhabitants, too,
abandoned [Mt] Xoburgo and
came down to the harbour, where
they adjusted to the new
conditions of life and the demands
of growing commercial activity.
The period of insecurity was past,
and the new town gathered in the
raw silk and wine from the villages
for export, along with the products
of the cottage industries: silk
stockings, scarves, gloves and
basketware.'

'The Venetians are said to have
brought doves to Tinos, and to
have been the only ones who had
the right to keep them on their
property. The villagers, as serfs of
the Venetians, built the dove-cotes
that did not belong to them and
tended doves that were not their
own. It was only when the
Venetians departed in the 18th
century and the villagers became
masters of their own land, that

they built countless dove-cotes of
their own throughout the island; a
conservative estimate puts the
present total at one
thousand...What is certain is that
on Tinos, the simple birds' house
became a superb example of
vernacular architecture. In the
cornfields, and in the
vegetable-gardens of the river
valleys, the craftsmen built elegant
rectangular two-storey buildings
with a flat roof and an upper roof
surmounted by abstract
three-dimensional compositions
made of thin slabs of unworked
schist. The small windows through
which the birds came and went
formed the basis for the superb
decoration that adorned the walls.
The thin slabs of schist framing the
holes spread in schematic patterns
over the entire surface of the walls,
in the countless shapes and motifs
beloved by the sensitive
craftsmen.'
ANGELIKI KHARITONIDOU

ABOVE The island of Tinos, on the northeastern periphery of the Cyclades, has been, since the nineteenth century, Greece's answer to the shrine of Lourdes. Every summer, concurrent with the country's hottest weather and at the height of the tourist season, the Orthodox faithful flock to the island on a pilgrimage to the *Megalohari,* or 'The Great and Gracious Lady,' the wonder-working icon of the Virgin Mary that was discovered here by a workman on 30 January 1823. The annual feast of the Assumption of the Virgin begins on 15 August and ends, with the Novena of The Virgin, on 23 August. The sick, the lame and the infertile alike all crowd into the town, all hoping to be granted a cure by the Virgin. The focus of this journey of hope and faith is the Church of The *Panagheia Evangelistria,* or Lady of Good Tidings.

ABOVE, RIGHT AND OPPOSITE
'Votive offerings, found throughout the world and in all periods of history, are presented for a variety of reasons: the granting of a wish, the cure of an illness, the safe birth of a child, or for divine intercession in personal affairs or a catastrophe such as an automobile accident, a shipwreck or an earthquake. In return, an offering—a tama—is made to express—before or after the fact—thankfulness and devotion... These tamata become the property of the church where they are dedicated. In the past, some were made of silver or gold and were ultimately melted down to be made into goblets or candelabra... Tamata could thus be an important source of income for a church and, ...in Tinos, contribute significantly to the economic welfare of the community...'
BRUCE BATLER AND JULIA GRANT

'It was a fine starry night, and the thousands of little oil lamps which decorated the church and its steeple rivalled the lights of the celestial hemisphere in their twinklings. Patience, assisted now and again by an ingenious push, enabled us to get inside and witness the weird sights in the church—men and women were there grovelling on their knees; cripples, blind and halt, were imploring the favour of the Madonna; further on, a woman, after standing ominously still for a while, as if contemplating the scene, was suddenly seized with religious frenzy. She shrieked, she threw her arms about, and was carried out in wild hysteria. This frenzy was most infectious, and presently the whole church was full of hideous yells and maddened suppliants who are supposed when in this state to be under the special influence of the Deity. There is something which carries one's mind back to Antiquity in the way these crowds are lodged. In olden days no inns existed on Delos, and at the festivals places of shelter were found near and in the temple. Now in Tinos the old custom of incubatio is continued, for when invalids aspire to a perfect cure they must sleep in the church…'

J. T. BENT, 1885

'The Orthodox Church venerates the Virgin Mary as "more honorable than the cherubin and beyond compare more glorious than the seraphim," as superior to all created beings. The Church sees in her the Mother of God, who, without being a substitute for the One Mediator, intercedes before her Son for all humanity.'
SERGIUS BULGAKOV

'In the ninth century St Theodore the Studite, one of the most articulate defenders of the cult of sacred images, used the metaphor of a signet ring impressed into various sealing media to help demonstrate the instability of the icon: "The impression is one and the same," he wrote, "...yet it would not have remained identical unless it were entirely unconnected with materials...[and] the same applies to the likeness of Christ, irrespective of the material upon which it is represented." His point was that the icon as a palpable "thing" effectively disappears as it becomes a mediating devotional vehicle (a "door") between the venerating beholder and the deity or saint represented.'
GARY VIKAN

'Little enough remains now save the chain of ruined forts, and the names of famous battles petrifying slowly in the history-books. The culture to which the Knights were heirs took shallow roots which barely outlived their departure. It never penetrated to the heart of the Mediterranean way-of-life—that mixture of superstition, impulse and myth which so quickly grows up around whatever is imported, seeking to domesticate it. The landscape puts her nymphs arms about the human habits, beliefs, styles of mind so that imperceptibly they are overgrown by the fine net of her caresses—paths choked with weeds, wells blocked by a fallen coping-stone, fortresses silvered over with moss. Decay superimposes its own chaos, so that standing on some heap of stones today, watching a shepherd milk his goats, hearing the drizzle of milk in the cans chimed by the whizz of the gnats which hover round him, you wonder whether this mauled assembly of stones is Frankish or Mycenean, Byzantine or Saracen. Often enough the answer is: all of these. But only the eye of a specialist can read it like a palimpsest, text imposed on text, each dedicated to its peculiar folly or poetry.'
LAWRENCE DURRELL

Symi contributed three vessels to the Trojan campaign, was colonized by the Carians, who found it inhospitably arid, and was later dishonoured by the Lacedaemonians who, after defeating an Athenian fleet off Knidos, erected a trophy on the island. Symi's shipbuilders supplied the Knights of St John, then the Turks and, following them, the Greek patriots of the Revolutionary War. Today, in the harbour of Yialos, they continue to practice their ancient craft.

'The self-contained and partly hidden water-borne local trade of the Levant has existed for centuries and even millennia, but its patterns, routes and centres have shifted in response to political, technological or natural developments. In ancient times, Rhodes supplanted Delos as a centre of the Aegean shipping trade. In the modern era, before the Greek War of Independence (1821–1832), Psara and Chios were among the most important Aegean seaports, trading and shipbuilding centres, along with Symi, Rhodes, Hydra and Spetses.'
PAUL WINROTH

OPPOSITE, ABOVE AND OVERLEAF The island of Karpathos, second largest of the Dodecanese, lies between Crete and Rhodes. A long, steep sliver of rock, it is 48 kilometres (30 miles) long, but only 11 kilometres (7 miles) wide, encompassing some 859 square kilometres (332 square miles) of land. Saria, an islet off the northern tip of Karpathos, is home today to only a few shepherds, and Karpathos itself is still little-visited. Off the main tourist routes, it has been able to preserve its rich and colourful cultural heritage far longer than its more cosmopolitan neighbours. The renowned forests of Karpathos, which led a fifteenth-century traveller to remark that Karpathians were dark because they extracted pitch from their trees, have largely disappeared. The remaining pines are located in the centre of the island, though Karpathos's formerly agricultural economy—its army of windmills now sail-less—has altered dramatically in the last century, due to the advent of a money economy and widespread emigration. The village of Olimbos (or Elymbos) is situated to the north of the island beneath Mt Profitis Elias, once called the Karpathian Olympus. This region, inhabited in antiquity, gave rise to the village between the ninth and the fifteenth centuries. The original Olimbians were either shepherds drawn from the surrounding area, or the displaced populace of Vrykounta, a village further north which was destroyed by earthquake, who resettled here. Originally a strongly fortified settlement, built amid lush pine-covered hills and plentiful vegetation, Olimbos is now stranded on an arid, rocky ridge.

'In its remoteness the village of Olymbos (pronounced "Elimbos" by the natives) has maintained its way of life through all vicissitudes and has held on to its ancient traditions. A road connecting it with the southern part of the island was only completed in 1979. Electricity arrived in 1981, and two years ago the village still had only one telephone. Changes are coming, but many things remain unchanged. Music and dance are among the best preserved living traditions of the village. Here, the same instruments—lyra with small bells attached to the bow, laouto, tsambouna (a form of bagpipe)—are played just as they have been for generations. Fortunately, the music has not been tainted by bouzouki, electric organ and drums as in so many forms of traditional Greek music. So akin are the scales and style to the Byzantine that some may mistake folk music for ecclesiastic. Unlike many parts of Greece today, Olymbos abounds with musicians, though none truly professional. A shoemaker plays laouto; a coffee house owner, tsambouna; a farmer, lyra; the postman, lyra and laouto; and students studying medicine or law or dentistry abroad may play a variety of instruments.'

YVONNE HUNT

'The extreme remoteness of the area until very recently explains why it is better known to folklorists and philologists than to historians. The unique local dialect has retained many elements of ancient Doric which has attracted linguists from all over the world since the last century. Women still wear the traditional forms of dress, not just for festive occasions as in most parts of Greece, but as everyday wear. For this reason the women of Olymbos can often be identified in Piraeus and even, occasionally, in Athens. Upon entering the village by way of its steep stairways—there are no streets—one is immediately impressed by the blue, yellow, beige-rose colours of the houses, a palette of pastel hues. Many of the houses have imaginatively carved and painted balconies decorated with folk motifs or the double-headed eagle, symbol of the Byzantine Empire. The interiors are distinguished by a soufas, a raised, elaborately carved area used as sleeping quarters for the whole family. Here, where traditional embroidering and fine weavings are displayed, unmarried girls once silently watched celebrations when they were held indoors, but never participated in them. Above, shelves hold the plates, jugs and other ceramics brought home by men who had found work in Turkey, the Arab countries or other Greek islands.'

YVONNE HUNT

'At a typical panigyri [saint's day feast], following the liturgy and the communal meal (in the case of the many family-owned churches, the owners provide everything), the men, separated from the women, start to sing. Perhaps several hours later, the men begin to dance the Kato Horos while singing mantinades for a particular saint, or, if at a wedding, for the bride and groom. These rhymed couplets, melancholy or happy, are impromptu and spontaneous. Now women slowly join in the dance, the positions of the young girls in the line chosen by their mothers and never by chance. Although women alternate with men at first and a preponderance of women often fill the end of the line, it is always led and closed by men. The Kato Horos may last several hours before the most beloved dance of the elimbites begins, the Pano Horos, and its variation, the Sousta. This dance demands immense stamina, for it is vigorous and may last without stopping for three days, reverting back to mantinades and the Kato Horos when the dancers begin to slow down a bit. The musicians change every now and then but never with a break in the music. One musician slides into a chair as the other rises out of it. Dancers may drop out as they tire, perhaps to sleep for an hour or two before returning, but there are always those who are refreshed to take their place.'

YVONNE HUNT

ABOVE AND LEFT *'When the dough is ready I make the sign of the Cross over it, cut off a little to keep for my prozimi [starter] and shape the rest into six or seven large loaves. Each loaf will be placed in one of the slots of the* pinacoti *[hollowed-out beam] and covered with the* messali, *a long white towel. The pinacoti is left in a dark room with one or two blankets heaped on top to help the dough rise. In the meantime I busy myself with the other household chores for about an hour. Then I begin to heat my oven. I stuff it first with thin dry twigs that will burn quickly, and then I add one or two large pieces of wood. The oven must heat up evenly. Kneading and baking take up a lot of my time… but I feel that it's worth the extra work because homemade bread tastes better.'*

YEORYIA KOSMA

In the village of Lefkos, on Karpathos, on 23 April, villagers celebrate the nameday of the saint at the Church of St George. The priest in his sunny vestments censes the holy bread, which is cut and distributed to the celebrants. The silver-chased icon of the horseman-saint is banked with spring flowers, and watched over by a member of the congregation, as the faithful bend to kiss their patron's image.

'St George, the Knight on the white horse, is among the most popular saints of Greece, and his feast is kept throughout the country. More than any other saint, perhaps, St George is the incarnation of the ideal hero of antiquity. The hymns written for him incorporated at an early stage several ancient legends, and have thus caused him to be associated with the demigods and heroes of ancient Greek mythology. In the Middle Ages the figure of St George adorned the banners and pennons of the Byzantine Emperors, and it figures to this day on the regimental flags of the Greek Army of which he is the patron saint. The miraculous exploits of St George—how he slew the Dragon and rescued the Princess thrown as a prey to the beast in order to let the waters of the city run free—are vividly related in a popular song familiar to every Greek. In some parts of Greece the elements of this song have even infiltrated into the customs of popular worship. Thus at Arachova, near Mount Parnassus—a village under the protection of the Saint—the evening service and procession during which his icon is carried round the village, are followed by dancing to the sound of bagpipes and drums; the dance is led by the old men of the village... The shepherds of Greece pay St George special homage. The reason for this is probably that his nameday coincides with the time when shepherds and flocks leave the folds and move up to the mountain pastures.'
GEORGE A. MEGAS

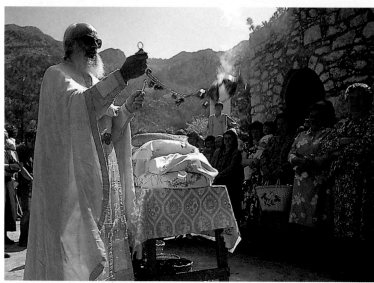

CRETE

CRETE IS OUR ANCESTRAL HOME; THE MINOAN FRESCOES, OUR common coat of arms. It is the island motherland where European civilization first flowered and where no Westerner ever visits as a 'simple' tourist, for it was in the peaceful courtyards of the ruler we call Minos, that our notions of religion, of government and commerce, of the arts and architecture, were forged as long ago as the 3rd millenium BC. It was on Crete, the rocky wall that separates Europe from Africa—that linked Europe *to* Africa and Asia—that our first recognizably 'Western' graffiti were elegantly painted. The southernmost sector of Greece became the foundation of the pyramid, the firm pediment upon which we all, as Mycenaean and Periclean Greeks, as Romans, Byzantines and Latins, as Europeans, Americans, and Moderns of all cultures and creeds, have built. Europe's most ancient road was laid at Knossos, and it survives to this day—a path we have all taken. We are all, in a very real sense, Cretans.

In very ancient times, this island was a kind of Eden. In the Upper Pleiocene period, Crete was made up of four separate isles. It was once home to antelope, deer, hippopotami and dwarf elephants, and the rare, endangered *agrimi,* or *kri-kri* goat of Crete, the last of the island's fauna to walk across the vanished land bridge from Asia, was well-settled on the island when the first human immigrants arrived from southwest Asia in *c.* 6,500 BC. These pilgrim-fathers of Europe found a forest-paradise far removed from the tree-poor, stony island we see today. Crete was called 'fair and fertile' by Homer, and 'the garden of the whole Universe' as late as 1609, by the traveller William Lithgow during his visit to Chania. Today, it is characterized by barren and sun-bleached limestone massifs, its fertile pockets and plains intensely cultivated. It was the Venetians, with their greedy axes, who began the cycle of erosion now so familiar on Crete, and it is the seedling-hungry goats of Crete themselves that continue the process, stripping bare Crete's mountainous slopes.

It is Crete's mountains which first strike the visitor. The tortuous vertebrae of the Lefka Ori, or 'White Mountains', stabbing through blue haze, are the first visible evidence of the so-called 'Great Island' after the long voyage south from Piraeus. Five great massifs divide the island like the bones of some fallen, archaic god. Significantly, it was in Crete's mountains that Zeus, the father of the Olympians himself, was born and reared. Island legend has long had it that above Irakleion, on Mt Youktas, Zeus still lies entombed, his martial profile and war helmet slicing into the urban sky. But though the teeming, modern cities of Irakleion, Chania, Rethymnon, Aghios Nikolaos and Siteia all reflect the island's post-war prosperity, Crete has only known peace for a short half-century. Old ways die hard but on Crete, the old ways never die. It has always been to the mountains that Cretans have looked for their gods, and for salvation. The mountains, unlike Crete's conquerors and fickle allies down through history, have never disappointed and never betrayed.

The Sfakianes Madares range in the west, the central Ida massif and the Dikte or Lassithi mountains, the Asterousia to the south, and the eastern Siteian range—these peaks are the Cretans' true home; the only place where they feel truly comfortable. They are the impenetrable sanctuary where the fierce and uncompromising islanders have sought protection from oppression throughout centuries of invasion. After the fall of the great, Minoan civilization, Crete would never again give rise to a peaceful, 'unfortified' culture. Such follies as rich palaces bordering an unprotected littoral, where treasures were not locked away behind bolted doors and where princes strutted about in fine plumage, their traditional crossed sabers or muskets abandoned—these would be looked upon as sheer madness on post-Minoan Crete.

Upon the fall of Knossos, and the other peace-loving palaces, all Cretans forsook their treacherous shores for the hills. Only the deep and dangerous ravines of Sfakia and the secluded and fertile plateaux beyond the mountain passes, could offer the beseiged any respite from colonizer and pirate. It was in the mountains that the Cretans developed the distinctive way of life—and way of looking at life—that survives on the island today. In the words of Nikos Kazantzakis—the Cretan author whose life spanned the Ottoman occupation, World War Two and the Greek Civil War, and whose literary career was largely given over to describing what he has called the 'Cretan glance'—Crete's maxim has always been 'freedom or death'.

'I gazed at the bullfights painted on the walls: the woman's agility and grace, the man's unerring strength, how they played with the frenzied bull, confronting him with intrepid glances. They did not kill him out of love in order to unite with him, as in oriental religions, or because they were overcome with fear and dared not look at him. Instead, they played with him, obstinately, respectfully, without hate. Perhaps even with gratitude. For this sacred battle with the bull... cultivated... the valor—so difficult to acquire—to measure his strength against the beast's fearful power without being overcome by panic.'
– Nikos Kazantzakis, *Report to Greco*, trans. by Peter Bien.

Kazantzakis's autobiography, *Report to Greco*, is a distillation of Cretan history and Cretan wisdom, largely transmitted to the author as a young man by the island's grand old men, the centenarians, and their octogenarian sons, who fought the Venetians, the Turks, and the Egyptians. Their own forefathers had faced other invaders just as ferociously; their grandsons would defeat the Germans. Today's old men, Kazantzakis's contemporaries, can still be found sitting in the village *kafeneia* (cafés), wearing their *vraka*, the baggy, blue trousers with their elephantine seats, or *sela*, belted by a *zounari*, or sash, which is traditionally some eight metres (26 feet) long. Their knee high boots, or *stivalia*, like those still made by cobblers in the old quarter of Rethymnon, are white or black. Their beetling brows are fringed by a black kerchief, whose knotted hem dangles before hard, black eyes. Even younger men in the mountains still borrow components of this pre-industrial age garb: it was custom-made for men who climbed the Cretan outback in search of flocks or foes. But even without the costume, the Cretan mystique still hangs about the young who live above sea level on Crete. Honour, throughout the island, is as important a 'garment' today as it was in Nikos Kazantzakis's boyhood, though trigger-happy fingers now are not quite so restless.

In the package-holiday towns on the northern littoral, where drunken teenagers from northern Europe reel today, and topless bathers parade on the sand, there is no trace of Kazantzakis's Crete. Depopulated and desperately poor through the 1960s, the island was in dire need of the foreign exchange injected by its summer guests, and Cretan hoteliers and *taverna* owners are only too happy to welcome the windfall profits brought by tourism over the last two decades. But visitors will be in grave error if they mistake this flimsy development on the shore for Crete itself. Crete took to the hills in the fifteenth century BC, and remains there, its traditional houses unchanged in structure since the Minoan era, its music and poetry based on a philosophy of resistance and heroism that has no time for lying in the sand or frolicking in the surf. In the villages of the hills and mountains, where no beaches or bars entice the tourists or corrupt the Cretans, the lifestyle has withstood centuries of threats far more violent than those posed by this late-twentieth-century crusade.

On Crete, and throughout all of Greece, what is most Greek is no longer to be found where the beach awning has been raised, and the 'Wine Tasting Evening' is touted. Faced for so many centuries with invaders, the Greeks have learned to leave for the plunderer what he seeks, and to retreat with the real valuables. And if the Greek can be richly paid for the things left behind, things he feels, for the most part, to be worthless, so much the better. The Cretan beaches he will cede to Athenian developers and Cretan businessmen—for a price—but his daughters are rarely offered in marriage to the 'foreigners' (from Athens and Munich, alike), his village real estate is largely not for sale, and the 'Cretan glance' he reserves for other Cretans. In this way only can the Cretan obey the legendary laws of Cretan hospitality, extending a hand to the stranger in utmost generosity, and still preserve, in the other hand, for Nikos's grandchildren, and great-grandchildren, the precious, blood-spattered rock that is Crete.

PAGE 152: 'Crete is a land of
tremendous scenic gestures,
emphatic and innocent. It strikes
one at once with its breadth and
magnificence. It is not a peaceful
landscape but a tumultous one,
fully orchestrated. We seem
incapable of embracing directly
the totally new, but must approach
it obliquely for safety. And so I
sought to relate the effect of Crete
upon me to something else in my
experience. Only music, I think,
can translate the spirit in the same
way as Crete does. The most
gorgeous sound I know is a fanfare
of silver trumpets sounding when
an orchestra has fallen silent. But
in this landscape of mountainous
distances the sound of those
trumpets is quite mute, their note
has passed into vibrations beyond
registration by our ears. Yes,
broad, in its magnificent sense, is a
word for Crete… Crete offers
unending vistas of excess. Deserts
which can give one spiritual
refreshment by their offering of
inexhaustible repose, are able to
compensate one for not being a
hero. But Crete challenges one to
attain a greater stature, it seems to
promise this if, after all, one can
achieve the hero's stamina. This
challenge, which the landscape
itself seems to throw out, is not for
the visitor alone. The Cretans
themselves acknowledge it and
much of the visitor's pleasure is
due to the spirited way in which
they accept it. Generation after
generation takes it up and it is the
touchstone by which they live.'
CHRISTOPHER KININMONTH, 1949

At the Minoan palace of Knossos, outside Irakleion, the so-called Grand Staircase clearly reflects archaeologist Sir Arthur Evans' philosophy of excavation and imaginative reconstruction. The British scholar had a very personal, and controversial vision of Minoan civilization, and his extensive and colourful refurbishments of Bronze Age columns and frescoes have drawn fire for a century. First discovered by a Cretan with the portentous name of Minos Kalokairinos, the site was initially offered to another archaeologist, Heinrich Schliemann. Though Kalokairinos had found only large storage *pithoi* when the Turks got wind of the dig, Schliemann was renowned for finding gold. His fame as the excavator of Mycenae and Troy inflamed the Ottoman's greed, and they priced Knossos above the German scholar's means. The Turks left Crete in 1899, however, and Evans was then allowed to take over the excavation. Settled since *c.* 6,000 BC, the structure we see today is actually the Second Palace. The original fell in an earthquake in *c.* 1,700 BC, was subsequently rebuilt, and later occupied by Greeks from the mainland–Mycenae, to be precise–after *c* 1,450 BC.

'No Greek story is more familiar than that of how Minos ruled the waves (a tradition, in which Herodotos and Thucydides believed as history); how he took Nisa, the predecessor of the city of Megara, and took tribute of Athens in revenge for the murder of his son, in the form of seven youths and seven maidens each year to be fed to his monstrous beast, the Minotaur; and how Prince Theseus volunteered to be one of them and slew the Minotaur, by the help of Ariadne, Minos' daughter, who fell in love with him and gave him the Clue–a literal clue, a ball of wool to unwind behind him–with which to find his way back out of the labyrinth. But only since the archaeological discoveries has it been noticed how many elements in the story seem to be garbled reminiscences of facts about ancient Crete.

A. R. AND MARY BURN

'The harbour is delightful. Its inner recesses are backed by a row of splendid Venetian arsenals, great vaulted sheds for building and mending galleys in, now used, spasmodically, for storage only. (A very nasty hotel, all concrete balconies, was erected here in 1973.) But the best part of the harbour is the little three-quarter circle by the sea entrance. A Venetian-Egyptian lighthouse stands on the mole. Fishing boats ride on the landward side, made fast to the edge of a road which is backed by houses more beautiful still than those at Rethimnon. Few modern buildings have so far intruded and the style is unmistakably Venetian. There is a lovely stairway rising to first-floor level on the back of a half-arch—an architectural feature often found in Greece. At one end of the harbour circle stands a purpose-built mosque converted into a tourist information office and shiny restaurant; at the other end, restored and painted a deep puce, a mansion which houses a naval museum. It is a child's paradise, full of models of ships, real bits of torpedoes and portraits of the bearded admirals of Greece's modern wars. Between these two extremes are restaurants serving the best food in Crete... The district on the little hill above the maritime museum—only a few steps from the harbour front—consists of alleys often not much wider than an armspan. The houses rise high, reminding one of Naples, and, as in Naples, everything is peeling and misshapen.'

ADAM HOPKINS

'Khania, the second city of Crete at the time of the Venetians, is now its capital… It is an over-crowded town, as it was at the time of the Venetians, from the narrowness of the streets, the height of some of the houses and the confined limits of the original plan… In looking towards the south from the bay…the peaks of the noble mass of the Madra Vouna, the ancient Leuci or White Mountains, rise most picturesquely before one in a serrated arch…'
CAPTAIN T. A. B. SPRATT, 1865

PREVIOUS PAGE At Irakleion, the harbour is guarded still by a sixteenth-century Venetian fortress. Crimson nets are piled to dry in the vaulted arsenals. For two decades, the Venetians and their allies held out against the Turks here, but on 5 September 1669, Francesco Morosini surrendered. Irakleion, under the Ottomans, became known as the *Megalo Kastro,* the Great Castle.

ABOVE AND RIGHT Cretan knives are the stuff of legend. At this *Mahairopoieïon,* or knifemaker's shop, in Chania, Mr Spanouthakis (identifiable as a Cretan by his surname's suffix-akis) displays a pair of blades attached to the horns of the Cretan goat, the *kri-kri.* Cretan knives were traditionally etched with short, fierce, rhyming poems. In Neapolis, another mustachioed islander practices a far more peaceful craft. He fashions the large goats' bells, or *kriarakoudouna,* so beloved of Skyros's 'goat dancers'.

ABOVE AND LEFT Mr Alkis Skoulas, the naïf painter and sculptor of Anoghia, depicts Crete's heroic history in primitive oils and woodcarvings. His son carries on another tradition of Cretan artistry: folk balladry accompanied by the Cretan *lyra*. Anoghia, the island's largest mountain village, is today a prosperous centre of weaving and embroidery, where many homes contain massive, traditional looms, and residents still wear their native dress. The accent of Anoghians, and much of their dialect have their roots in antiquity: the village has survived many centuries of Crete's turbulent history. In fact, in August 1941, Anoghia was razed to the ground, its inhabitants massacred, in a brutal act of reprisal by the Germans under General Müller.

'For two and a half months we lived in Khania, moving from house to house. Our main hiding place, to which we returned frequently, was the home of Mitsos Antonakakis and his wife Artemisia, near the harbour. They welcomed us as their sons, and here I began to learn the hospitality and the courage of the Cretan people. They showed us how to escape if the Germans should come to the house, knowing full well that they could not escape themselves, and that they and their family would certainly be shot. Behind them, with this same hospitality and courage, stood the whole Cretan people, ready to hide British soldiers after the German invasion, and to help us in the resistance regardless of the danger...'
STEPHEN VERNEY

'A housewife's major, ongoing task is to love and tend her co-resident kin, both children and adults. She performs this task daily, although, since formal education became compulsory in 1967, the school provides some of the care of children. Each day, a woman also fetches water, sweeps, cooks one main and two minor meals, and, depending on need, sews, weaves, spins, gardens, or collects brushwood for the bread oven. Every ten days to two weeks, she bakes bread. Once a month she may wash clothes and split wood in the courtyard. Every couple of months, she washes and beats the rugs at a village tap… Women bear heavy burdens, lauding their own efforts and strength; they work unceasingly and boast of their fatigue. Claiming that only old, weak women need long handled brooms, they sweep the floor with brooms that are only three feet long…Even as household pride makes for straight backs, women's sweat makes for bent ones. Their stouthearted exhaustion communicates to the young not only how to suffer well, but also how to struggle well; how to cope with the need to work hard in a hard world; and how to resist the personal erosion that comes from grappling with hard work.'
MURIEL DIMEN

'You see I wear black. But it isn't only the clothes I wear which are black. My man is dead. In the house of your mother, father, sisters, brothers, you are a guest [mousafiri]; you are an outsider [xeni]. You live with them, but you are an outsider. But with your man you are a nikokyra [mistress of the house]. When you are a nikokyra no one says you didn't do this right, or come and eat this food which was made for you. I don't have my own household. I don't have anything anymore.'
78-YEAR-OLD WIDOW
(QUOTED BY ROBINETTE KENNEDY)

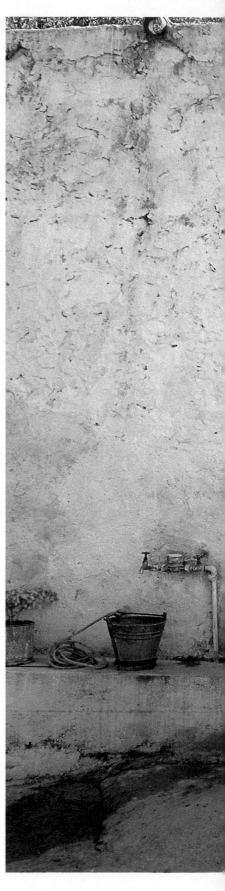

'The old woman of eighty or ninety, who spends the winter months curled on the corner of a striped divan near the stove and emerges in the summer to sit on a stool or balcony or doorstep, carries memories of a life punctuated by war and political turbulence. As she dandles her grandchildren and great-grandchildren she is certain that the one thread that runs through all external events is family. But while she has a powerful sense of continuity, which, no doubt, she tries to instil into the generations that follow after, she lives in a world where the very substance of life has been transformed. If, as is likely, she started life in a small village (the cities and major towns all expanded during the course of this century), she will have seen the peasant's daily *aghona* (struggle) in the fields transmuted into something more like a regular day's work. Women's labor in the fields is still a very significant part of the Greek economy… But it is unlikely to be the intensively heavy work which broke down the health of women in the early part of the century and, very often endangered their babies too. The coming of the *trakter*, the pride of the farming man, bedizened with necklaces like a favorite horse, has freed women's bodies for lighter labor… Greek women's handiwork is no mere pastime. It is bound closely to the traditional sense of woman's role and destiny. A young girl learns to sew so that she will be marriageable. These skills symbolize, obscurely, all that she must be. The bride must show that she has the wherewithal to "dress" the house, all the ornamental and comfortable fabrics which will line the nest of marriage. The usually impressive accumulation of fabrics and furnishings is brought to the new house with some ceremony—in the past on the backs of a string of well laden mules, now more often in a truck which creeps through village or neighborhood with the horn sounding…'
LUCY RUSHTON

In the Old Garden

After many years, the sick woman got up,
went into the garden. Winter
sunshine. Enclosed serenity—
on it float the thud of nails driven
into new, invisible
scaffoldings. The grass is fragrant.
Flower-pots, terraces,
eaten away by hairy plants and
roots. The pomegranate tree
taller than the cypress. The well
closed. Yellow dust
like the dust that falls behind icons
full of holes. And suddenly
the distant, nuptial smell of cool
orange-blossoms
beautifully arranged around a
silver tray
on the pedestal of a proud statue
that is absent.
YANNIS RITSOS,
TRANS. BY N. C. GERMANACOS

Villagers' homes, where water is available, become leafy bowers, sanctuaries of aromatic herbs, flowering shrubs and fruit trees. Planted and tended as much for a family's guests as for the family itself, these areas, enclosed by whitewashed olive-oil tins brimming with geraniums and lilies, serve as sleeping quarters and dance floors in summer, when saints' days and family festivities such as baptismal parties or engagements, are celebrated out-of-doors. Simple, wooden chairs softened with ruffled cushion covers; a tin *ikonostasis* in which a saint's icon and oil lamp are on view; and a humble table set with tiny glasses of *tsigoudia*, or *ouzo*, and *koulourakia*, sweet biscuits, all indicate the occupants' reverence for tradition, and traditional love of their guests. *Philoxenia*, or 'love of strangers', is a time-honoured tenet of Greek culture, and nowhere is it more lavishly expressed than in rural Crete. With the air scented with basil, mint, lemon blossom and roses, the guest is invited to partake of a 'spoon sweet', or fruit compote, prepared by the women of the house, then offered a liqueur and Greek coffee, followed by a glass of cool water. On Crete, visitors should not be surprised to be offered the best chair in the house, the family's bed, a meal, and anything else the villager can think of to make the guest more comfortable. And, though Cretan gallantry and generosity in the developed north are eroding due to the floods of summer visitors, in the hill and mountain villages, *philoxenia* remains the most characteristic of Cretan virtues.

'The nomadic life of the inhabitants of the mountainous stock-raising villages, as well as the agricultural ones at lower levels, made the transfer of furniture difficult, so it was limited to the bare minimum. The basic furniture, such as the ledge or the sofas for sleeping, the thyrides for small objects and the laïnostatis to hold the water jug were built at the same time as the house so that by the time the house was finished it was practically ready to be lived in. For eating they used a low, round table, the sofras, and low stools or chairs. The most basic piece of furniture in the Cretan house, particularly in the kamarospito [flat-roofed house with a supporting arch], was the long divan which was situated opposite the entrance and was used for receiving guests. The loom, the argastiri as they call it, was indispensible, for the housewife used it to weave all the materials the family needed, such as large red woollen blankets, rugs and bags. The dowry materials and clothing in general were stored in a chest with dried rose leaves. In the kitchen there was the alatsero, a cut-off gourd for salt, and the wooden spoon rack. In the laïnostatis the jug was placed on top of the astyvida [dry grass and shrub with thorns] and its mouth was closed with the stamnagathi [stopper made of brush]. The furnishing of the house was supplemented with various large clay jugs and olive oil jars.

PARASKEVI BOZINEKI-DIDONIS

ABOVE, AND OPPOSITE This rustic house which sits among labyrinthine lanes in a Cretan hill village was bought, a decade ago, by foreign visitors who had come to love the village and its inhabitants and wanted to spend Orthodox Easters and quiet summer holidays on Crete. The location of the village once provided protection from marauding pirates and it remains in peaceful seclusion. The visitors' respect for the Cretan way of life is reflected in the simple, spare interior; the possessions which seem familiar and appropriate to the family's Cretan neighbours. The red carpet is a traditional hand-woven design from Kritsa and the wicker-seated chairs are made by local craftsmen. Like the Cretans themselves, the household uses a low, round dining table and they have set out a plate of *koulourakia* for guests and, because it is Easter, a bowl of eggs dyed red, in memory of the blood of Christ. The humility and attention to detail exhibited here are not unusual among the small, valued ranks of expatriates who make Cretan villages their second homes. This is the reverse side of the devalued coin of modern tourism, and it is the kind of visitation encouraged by Cretan *philoxenia,* which establishes a reciprocal relationship of trust between Cretan hosts, and their foreign guests. Greeks are restoring houses in the village too, and there has been a recent influx of young Athenian artists.

PREVIOUS PAGE, OPPOSITE, TOP RIGHT
AND BOTTOM RIGHT Vangelis and
Theodoula Siligardos have been
making *raki,* the Cretan version of
Greece's *ouzo, tsipouro* and
tsigouthia, for all their married life.
The sternness of these Cretan
countenances and the reserve
displayed as they carry out this
demanding work, reflect the
respect felt for *raki* on Crete. It is
more than simply the national
drink, the Cretan schnappes.
Clear, fiery *raki* is the libation that
enlivens all Crete's festivities,
private and public, the first
offering to guests, the anaesthetic
applied to the gums of teething
Cretan babies, and the fuel that
makes long mountain treks and
freezing winter nights bearable.
Spyros Passias, discussing the
home production of *tsipouro* on
Pelion, gives an indication of what
forbearance and skill is required to
produce *raki:*

*'From grapes we produce wine as
well as* tsipouro. *Tsipouro is what
you get if you distill what remains
after the wine has been removed
from the barrel. Not everyone in
the village is allowed to make*
tsipouro. *Each producer has to get
a special permit from the Chemical
Board and the lid of every boiler
has to be registered with the
Municipality and the Police. Once
a year, for forty-eight hours, I am
allowed to unseal my lid and start
distilling. When the time is up, I
must bring the lid back to the
Police and have it sealed again.
During these forty-eight hours I
continue working non-stop, day
and night. It surely is a painful
task, what with the heat from the
fire and the fumes from the grapes,
but I've got my* tsipouro!'

OPPOSITE 'Days before our permit is due, we carry home large bunches of dried branches which we will use in the boiler. The fire has to be kept going, distilling one batch after another. When we are ready to begin, we spread an armful of dry twigs at the bottom of the boiler to prevent the dregs from sticking to the hot and burning metal. We then add one or two buckets of water. After this we place the lid on the boiler and seal the joint with a thin coat of mud made from white earth and bran.'
SPYROS PASSIAS

ABOVE Mrs Siligardos raises a glass of raki to the light to examine it for impurities. *Raki* must be perfectly clear, and she is pleased with the results. Cretan grape must yields not only wine and *raki,* but also pure alcohol, used for medicinal purposes, and must-fertilizer for flowers and crops. No part of the grape harvest is wasted.

'When the barrel is empty it must be thoroughly cleaned. The grower crawls inside and, using a hard brush and plenty of water, he scrubs it completely and then leaves it to dry. A few days before the next grape harvest, he starts wetting down the barrel twice a day to allow the wood to swell back to its original shape. He will get inside once again with a burner in one hand to scorch the inner surface with paraffin wax in order to seal any small cracks, just as a fisherman does before letting his boat into the water after the long winter months.'
HELEN-FAY STAMATI

*Fie on the young men down in the
plains Who taste the good things
of the world, the choicest foods,
And are base to look at like the
creeping lizard.
Joy to the young men up in the hills,
Who eat the snow and the
dew-fresh air And are fine to look at
like the orange tree.*
FROM M. LLEWELLYN-SMITH,
THE GREAT ISLAND

*The strong palikaria
Don't sleep at night;
But turn and turn in their
narrow space
And slash with their knives.*
CRETAN MANTINADE

'Two old men, one from Psychro and one from Magoulas, set themselves up along the main road between the two villages during the tourist season, wearing traditional male dress of baggy, Turkish style trousers and black headband. They offer themselves for photographs and then ask for money. Their summer life is probably far more entertaining than winter in the coffee house. Villagers are articulate in their criticism of this behaviour, however, and regard it as both selling oneself and begging for money. The old man from Magoulas does have yearnings of friendship towards the foreigners he meets (he is usually more or less ignored by the villagers and is always irritable with them). For the foreigners, however, he has a romantic appearance to offer, and would rather prostitute that than be left alone. Through the winter he brings letters and photographs from all over the world and expects me or my husband to translate them. He wants letters written in return inviting them to stay in his one-room house next summer, but seldom receives replies. The old man, and the tourists who photograph him, are trapped in their respective fantasies.'

SONIA GREGER

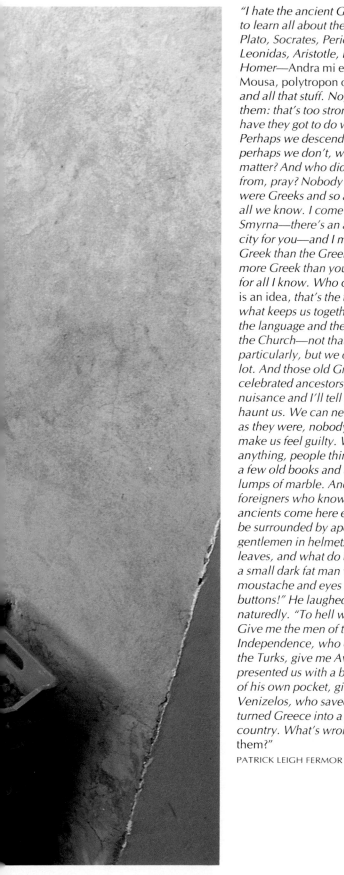

"I hate the ancient Greeks. We had to learn all about them at school: Plato, Socrates, Pericles, Leonidas, Aristotle, Euripides, Homer—Andra mi ennepe, Mousa, polytropon os malla polla and all that stuff. No, I don't hate them: that's too strong. But what have they got to do with me? Perhaps we descend from them, perhaps we don't, what does it matter? And who did they descend from, pray? Nobody knows. They were Greeks and so are we, that's all we know. I come from Smyrna—there's an ancient Greek city for you—and I may be more Greek than the Greeks in Athens, more Greek than your Sarakatsáns, for all I know. Who cares? Greece is an idea, that's the thing! That's what keeps us together—that, and the language and the country and the Church—not that I like priests particularly, but we owe them a lot. And those old Greeks, our celebrated ancestors, are a nuisance and I'll tell you why. They haunt us. We can never be as great as they were, nobody can. They make us feel guilty. We can't do anything, people think, because of a few old books and temples and lumps of marble. And clever foreigners who know all about the ancients come here expecting to be surrounded by apollos and gentlemen in helmets and laurel leaves, and what do they see? Me: a small dark fat man with a moustache and eyes like boot buttons!" He laughed good-naturedly. "To hell with them! Give me the men of the War of Independence, who chucked out the Turks, give me Averoff, who presented us with a battleship out of his own pocket, give me Venizelos, who saved us all and turned Greece into a proper country. What's wrong with them?"

PATRICK LEIGH FERMOR

'The shepherds… always have an air of independence and solitariness. They live a hard, spartan existence and appear to care more for the welfare of their sheep than for their own comfort. It is their stoical lifestyle which sets the ideal of powerful yet patient endurance for the whole village. Lambs are born mainly through autumn, most about October, but sometimes during the summer below. Most spend their first months at winter pasture. They return again in Spring, but snow remains on the high mountain until past Easter…'

'A fine Sunday in May, when all sheep are back on the mountain, is usually chosen for the sheep-shearing. Affines, cousins, etc., from other villages may be invited to help and this occasion is like a festival. All participants leave the village at dawn, for the walk up the mountain to pastures and sheep folds takes a good hour… On arrival at the hut and fold we were given wine, pieces of cold meat, sardines to fork out of a tin, and pieces of bread. It was still very chilly. About fifteen to twenty people participated… and two sheep were killed before any work started. The slaughter had a strong ritual air, everyone watched… Immediately the carcass was hung up by the hind legs onto a wooden peg and within five minutes the animals were skinned.'

'All through the shearing, which lasted from about eight-thirty to about three pm, and during which up to two hundred and fifty sheep were handled, women handed wine, raki and water to the men, and small pieces of meat or bread to keep them going. Other jobs were being done at the same time back at the shepherd's hut. Cooking was over an open fire outside the hut; cheese at various stages of maturation was tended inside…We gathered wild green salad, reputedly high in iron and vitamins but difficult to gather.'
SONIA GREGER

In the village of Thrapsano, near Myrtia, such master-potters as Ioannis Moutzakis, assisted by his family and young apprentices, create the huge *pithoi* which have been used on Crete since Minoan times for the storage of wine and oil, as well as more modern ceramics. Much of the ware goes for sale abroad. The clay, locally available, is repeatedly sieved to assure a high standard of purity. After being watered and kneaded, the clay is kept under cloths, to prevent evaporation in the dry air, till needed. The axles of the great potter's wheels are set in pits in the ground; the wheels themselves are just above ground level. An apprentice in the pit turns the wheel while the master himself fashions the *pithos* or large planter on the wheel.

When the master achieves the form he wants, the pot is allowed to 'rest', but it must be doused regularly with water to keep it from cracking. The last touch is the addition of the rolled rim, prepared by the potter's assistant. The fire, stoked by handfuls of sawdust, is kept at an even temperature. Quite close to the kiln, the temperature is almost unbearably hot, and the sawdust-throwers must alternate every quarter of an hour or so, especially in summer when the air temperature in Thrapsano rises to 38°C. As a visitor to the kilns, you will be treated with customary grace. Whether or not you make a purchase they are always pleased to display their craftsmanship, and you will be served coffee and *raki* by the master potter.

'Quickly from the priest's lighted candle the flame is passed. In a moment the dim building is illuminated by a lighted taper in every hand. A procession forms, a joyful procession now. Everywhere are light and glad voices and embraces of friends, crying aloud the news "Christ is risen!" and answering "He is indeed". In every home the lamb is prepared with haste, the wine flows freely; in the streets is the flash of torches, the din of firearms, and all the exuberance of simple joy. The fast is over; the dead has been restored to life before men's eyes; well may they rejoice even to ecstasy. For have they not felt the ecstasy of sorrow? It was all true, all real.'

C. LAWSON

'Good Friday is a day of total fast and abstention from work. Nearly the whole day is spent in attending the Descent from the Cross and the procession of the Epitaphios (Christ's funeral)… On Good Friday the Cretans eat boiled food mixed with vinegar, and boiled snails, for their juice resembles bile. In most villages the faithful do not even light a fire in their kitchen or put a mouthful to their lips…Towards noon, when the Descent from the Cross takes place, the womenfolk start decorating the pall (a piece of gold-embroidered cloth representing His body) upon which the dead Christ is to be placed. Each family in the village send their share of flowers for the decoration. Violets, roses, stocks, lemon-blossom—all the flowers of the spring—are woven into wreaths and bunches and pinned to the pall, until it is literally smothered in flowers… At nightfall the Epitaphios is carried out of the church, and the funeral procession begins. The banners and the Cross come first, followed by the Bier, which is in turn followed by the priests… The crowd following at the back hold candles made of pure brown wax; as the procession moves on, a broad flickering river seems to be streaming through the streets. The procession stops at every square and crossroad for the priests to say a short prayer… In several parts of Greece the villagers burn incense and light bonfires during the procession; it is not infrequent to see the effigy of Judas hoisted over the bonfire… The sorrowful gloom of Good Friday begins to lift on Holy Saturday with the evening service of the First Resurrection… Noisy scenes take place in the church, with the priest's participation, probably for the purpose of frightening away the demon who hovers over the congregation in order to hinder the Resurrection and the salvation of mankind.'
GEORGE A. MEGAS

'Loveliest of what I leave behind is
the sunlight,
and loveliest after that the shining
stars, and the moon's face,
but also cucumbers that are ripe,
and pears, and apples.
PRAXILLA OF SICYON
(TRANS. BY RICHARD LATTIMORE)

'A curious flower upon a fence had
caught our eye; we stopped to
pluck it. Children clustered around
us. "What do they call this
flower?" we asked. No one knew.
Then a dark haired little boy
jumped up: "Auntie Lenio will
know," he said. "Run and call
her," we told him. The little boy
ran off toward the town and we
waited holding the flower. We
admired it, sniffed it, but were
impatient; we longed for the word.
And then, in a short while, the boy
returned. "Auntie Lenio," he said,
"died the other day." Our hearts
constricted. We sensed that a
word had perished; perished and
now no one could place it in a
verse and render it immortal. We
were terrified. Never had death
seemed so irrevocable. And we
left the flower spread out on the
fence like a corpse.'
NIKOS KAZANTZAKIS
(QUOTED BY PETER BIEN)

'Whoever lives in this light, lives truly; with no aspiration, nostalgia, or grandezza, he lives. To live in the light—that is it. To leave this light, for existence among the shadows—that was the terrible, inconsolable thing. "Better to be a slave than Achilles here"—whoever has never seen this light cannot understand such a saying... I see from the top of a hill a few goats somewhere on a slope. The tinkling of their bells, the lifting of their heads, all this is real and yet at the same time as if drawn by the most inventive draughtsman. These creatures have in them something divine, something derived from the air, as well as something animal; this light is a ceaseless marriage of spirit and world. A steep cliff, a few pines, a small field of wheat, a tree whose aged roots cling to the rock full of crevices, a cistern, an evergreen shrub, a flower: the individual thing has no ambition to be merged into the whole, it is independent, but in this light independence is not the same as loneliness. Here if anywhere was the individual born, but to a divine and communal destiny. In this air one is wonderfully distinct—but one is not lonely, any more than any of the gods were ever lonely, whether they might appear from the waters or glide through the air, and here all creatures are gods. This pine, beautiful as a column of Phidias, is like a goddess. These spring flowers which scatter fragrance and sparkle down a sloping meadow—it has been said before, and rightly said: they stand there like little gods...'
HUGO VON HOFMANNSTHAL

INDEX

BIBLIOGRAPHY

Abbott, G. F. *Songs of Modern Greece.* Cambridge: Cambridge University Press, 1964.

Acheimastou-Potamianou, Myrtali, ed. *Holy Image, Holy Space: Icons and Frescoes from Greece.* Athens: Greek Ministry of Culture, 1988.

Agoropoulou-Birbilis, Aphrodite. *Corfu (Kerkyra).* Athens: Melissa Publishing House, 1984.

Agrafioti, Katerina. "Milies: a living tradition." *The Athenian* June 1988: 20-21.

Agrafioti, Katerina. "The Medici Secret." *The Athenian* December 1989: 34-36.

Agrafioti, Katerina. "Vathia: The Long Voyage Home." *The Athenian* October 1976: 28-30.

Agrafioti, Katerina. "Wearing Silver." *The Athenian* November 1990: 28-31.

"Albanians Reassure Mitsotakis." *Greek News* 19-25 January 1991: 3.

Allcorn, R. John. "Corcyra Illuminata: Isle of Enlightenment." *The Athenian* January 1991: 30-31.

Allen, Peter S. "Close-up of a Maniot Village." *The Athenian* October 1981: 21-24.

Andrews, Kevin. *Athens Alive, or The Practical Tourist's Companion to the Fall of Man.* Athens: Hermes Publications, 1979.

Andrews, Kevin. *The Flight of Ikaros.* Harmondsworth, Middlesex: Penguin Books, 1984.

Andronicos, Manolis. *Delphi.* Athens: Ekdotike Athenon S. A., 1984.

Arnaoutoglou, Chrysavgi. *Skyros.* Athens: Melissa Publishing House, 1984.

Aust, Michael. "Metsovo: Life Above Sea Level." *The Athenian* 12 April 1974: 19.

Barnard, Mary. *Sappho: A New Translation.* Berkeley and Los Angeles, California: University of California Press, 1958.

Batler, Bruce and Julia Grant. "A Custom From Ancient Times." *The Athenian* August 1978: 28-30.

Birrer, Richard. "The Underworld of Lavrion." *The Athenian* October 1979: 28-30.

Boleman-Herring, Elizabeth. "Travelling Light." *The Athenian* March 1990: 36-37.

Boleman-Herring, Elizabeth. "Travelling Light II: A Visit to the Meteora Continues." *The Athenian* April 1990: 35.

Boleman-Herring, Elizabeth. "Greek Unorthodox." Athens: Foundation Publishing, 1991.

Bouras, Charalambos. *Chios.* Melissa Publishing House, 1984.

Bowman, John S. "Minoan Mysteries." *The Athenian* July 1978: 20-24.

Bowman, John. "A Zoological Zorba: The Wild Goat of Crete." *The Athenian* January 1978: 20-24.

Bozineki-Didonis, Paraskevi. *Crete.* Athens: Melissa Publishing House, 1985.

Bulgakov, Sergius. *The Orthodox Church.* Syracuse, New York: St. Vladimir's Seminary Press, 1988.

Burn, A. R. *The Pelican History of Greece.* Thirteenth Impression. Harmondsworth, Middlesex, England: Penguin Books, 1983.

Burn, A. R. and Mary. *The Living Past of Greece.* Harmondsworth, Middlesex, England: Penguin Books, 1982.

Butterworth, Katharine M. "The Voice of the Turtle." *The Athenian* May 1989: 22-24.

Campbell, J. K. *Honour, Family and Patronage.* Oxford: Oxford University Press, 1964.

Cavarinos, Constantine. *Anchored in God: Life, Art, and Thought on the Holy Mountain of Athos.* Athens: Astir Publishing Company, 1959.

Chantiles, Vilma Liacouras. "Lunch in Metsovo." *The Athenian* June 1990: 40-41.

Christopoulos, Vassilis. *Achaia.* Athens: Melissa Publishing House, 1985.

Christou, Panagiotis K. *Athos, The Holy Mountain: History, Life, Treasures.* Thessaloniki: Kyromanos Publishers, 1990.

Clive, Nigel. *A Greek Experience: 1943-1948.* London: Michael Russell (Publishing) Ltd, 1985.

Clogg, Richard, ed. *Greece In The 1980s.* London: Macmillan Press Ltd, 1983.

Coulentianou, Joy. "The Misfits of Skyros." *The Athenian* May, 1981: 18-22; June 1981: 25-29.

Coulentianou, Joy. *The Goat-Dance of Skyros.* Athens: Hermes, 1977.

Coulson, Mary Lee. "Rebuilding 'the Rock.'" *The Athenian* October 1986: 26-28.

Dalven, Rae. *The Jews of Ioannina.* Philadelphia: Cadmus Press, 1990.

Delivorrias, Angelos, ed. *Greece and the Sea.* Athens: The Greek Ministry of Culture; The Benaki Museum, 1987.

Drinkwater, William J. "Symi and the liberation of the Dodecanese." *The Athenian* October 1985: 26-27.

Dubin, Marc S. "Back Country Trekking." *The Athenian* July 1984: 23-25.

Dubin, Marc S. *Greece On Foot, Mountain Treks, Island Trails.* Seattle: The Mountaineers, 1986.

Dubisch, Jill, ed. *Gender & Power in Rural Greece.* Princeton: Princeton University Press, 1986.

Durrell, Lawrence. *Prospero's Cell and Reflections on a Marine Venus.* New York: E. P. Dutton & Co., Inc., 1960.

Edwards, Grace. "Sacred Property of Andritsaina." *The Athenian* July 1981: 18-22.

Elliott, Sloane. "Archanes: Human Sacrifice in Minoan Crete." *The Athenian* March 1980: 22-30.

Elliott, Sloane. "La Belle Helene." *The Athenian* November 1976: 21-25.

Epirus and Ionian Islands Embroidery. Athens: Benaki Museum, 1965.

Eudes, Dominique. *The Kapetanios: Partisans and Civil War Greece, 1943-1949.* New York and London: Monthly Review Press, 1972.

Fafalios, Maria S. *Tales and Legends from Chios.* Athens, Akritas Publications, 1990.

Faltaits, Manos. *Skyros.* Athens: Northern Sporades Journal.

Foss, Arthur. *Epirus.* London: Faber and Faber Ltd, 1978.

Friar, Kimon and Kostas Myrsiades, ed. and trans. *Yannis Ritsos: Selected Poems, 1938-1988.* Brockport, New York: BOA Editions, Ltd., 1989.

Gage, Nicholas. *Hellas: A Portrait of Greece.* Athens: Efstathiadis Group, 1987.

Ginger, Stephanie and Christopher Klint. "Chios: The Chew in Chewing Gum." *The Athenian* January 1985: 26-27.

Greek Forest. Athens: The Goulandris Museum of Natural History, 1989.

Green, Sarah F. "Epirus: the living past." *The Athenian* October 1985: 30-33.

Greenhalgh, Peter and Edward Eliopoulos. *Deep Into Mani: Journey to the Southern Tip of Greece.* London: Faber and Faber Limited, 1985.

Gregor, Sonia. *Village on the Plateau,* Studley, Warwickshire: K.A. F. Brewin Books, 1988.

Gudas, Rom. "Tinos—island of the Sacred Icon." *The Athenian* March 1988: 22-27.

Hadjipateras, Costas N. and Maria S. Fafalios. *Crete 1941 Eyewitnessed.* Athens: Efstathiadis Group, 1989.

Hopkins, Adam. *Crete: Its Past, Present and People.* London: Faber and Faber, 1989.

Hunt, Yvonne. "The other Olympos." *The Athenian* June 1987: 24–27.

Huxley, George. *Homer and the Travellers: A Lecture on Some Antiquarian and Topographical Books in the Gennadius Library of the American School of Classical Studies at Athens.* Athens: 1988.

Igumen Chariton of Valamo, compiler. Ware, Timothy, ed. *The Art of Prayer: An Orthodox Anthology.* London: Faber and Faber Limited, 1985. (Note: this reprint translated by Elizabeth M. Palmer, 1966.)

Jenkins, Romilly. *Dionysius Solomos.* Athens: Denise Harvey & Company, 1981

Kadas, Sotiris. *Mount Athos: An Illustrated Guide to the Monasteries and Their History.* Athens: Ekdotike Athenon S.A., 1989.

Kalligas, Alexandros G. and Haris A. Kalligas. *Monemvasia.* Athens: Melissa Publishing House, 1986.

Karpodini-Dimitriadi, Efi. *The Peloponnese: A Traveller's Guide to the Sites, Monuments and History.* Athens: Ekdotike Athenon S. A., 1990.

Kazantzakis, Nikos. *Report to Greco.* P. A. Bien, trans. New York: Simon and Schuster, Inc, 1965.

Keeley, Edmund and Philip Sherrard. *Six Poets of Modern Greece.* London: Thames and Hudson, 1960.

Key, Elizabeth. "In the Central Pindus." *The Athenian* June 1990: 40-41.

Kharitonidou, Angeliki. *Tinos.* Athens: Melissa Publishing House, 1984.

Kininmonth, Christopher *The Children of Thetis.* London. 1949.

Kinnear, Angela. "Epirot Impasse: pollutants and protest." *The Athenian* March 1989: 19-21.

Klaus, Rainer W. and Ulrich Steinmuller. *Monemvasia: The Town and Its History.* Trans. by Lawrence P. Buck. Athens: 1980.

Komroff, Manuel, ed. *The History of Herodotus.* Trans. George Rawlinson. New York: Tudor Publishing Company, 1946.

Kouremenos, Kostas E. *The Sarakatsani.* Athens: Melissa Publishing House, 1985.

Leigh Fermor, Patrick. *Mani: Travels in the Southern Peloponnese.* London: John Murray, 1958.

Leigh Fermor, Patrick. *Roumeli: Travels in Northern Greece.* London: John Murray, 1966.

Lesser, Ellen. "Greece Through New Eyes." *The Athenian* October 1978: 22-25.

Leonidopoulou-Stylianou, Rea. *Pelion.* Athens: Melissa Publishing House, 1988.

Leventer, Lisa, ed. *The Penguin Guide to Greece: 1991.* New York: Penguin Books, 1991.

Lígeois, Jean-Pierre. *Gypsies: An Illustrated History.* London: Al Saqi Books, 1986.

Lord, Christopher. "Three-hearted castle: Oiniades." *The Athenian* November 1989: 28-31.

McIvor Kotsonis, Charles and John Haralambos Lewis. "To The Holy Mountain." *The Athenian* November 1978: 28-31.

Megas, George A. *Greek Calendar Customs.* Athens: B. and M. Rhodis, 1963.

Morris, Jan. *The Venetian Empire: A Sea Voyage.* London: Penguin Books, 1980.

Mylonas, George E. *Mycenae: A Guide to Its Ruins and Its History.* Athens: Ekdotike Athenon S. A., 1987.

Newby, Eric. *On the Shores of the Mediterranean.* London: Picador, Pan Books Ltd, 1985.

Pallis, A. A. *Greek Miscellany.* Athens, 1964.

Papantoniou, Ioanna. *Greek Costumes.* Nafplion: Peloponnesian Folklore Foundation, 1987.

Psaraki-Belesioti, Niki and Aemilia Yeroulanou. *Traditional Methods of Cultivation in Greece.* Athens: Benaki Museum Photographic Archive, 1978.

Paradissis, Alexander. *Fortresses and Castles of Greece, Volumes II and III.* Athens: Efstathiadis Group, 1982.

Patey, Katherine. "Endangered Forests." *The Athenian* November 1990: 18-22.

Petrakos, Basil. *National Museum: Sculpture, Bronzes, Vases.* Athens: Clio Editions, 1990.

Petrou Nikos. *Common Greek Birds.* Athens: The Goulandris Museum of Natural History, (undated).

Philippides, Dimitris. *Karpathos.* Athens: Melissa Publishing House, 1985.

Plomer, William. *The Diamond of Ioannina:*

Ali Pasha 1741-1822. New York: Taplinger Publishing Company, 1970.

Polunin, Oleg, and Anthony Huxley. *Flowers of the Mediterranean.* London: The Hogarth Press, 1987.

Pratt, Michael. *Britain's Greek Empire.* London: Rex Collins, 1978.

Provatakis, Theocharis M. *Meteora: History of the Monasteries and Monasticism.* Athens: Michalis Toumbis Editions, 1983.

Reid, William. "Glory Be to Goats." *The Southeastern Review* Summer 1990.

Rew, Dorene A. "The Horses of Greece: A Living Treasure." *The Athenian* December 1984: 35-37.

Rogoti-Kyriopoulou, Dimitra. *Yiannina.* Athens: Melissa Publishing House, 1989.

Romanos, Aristeidis. *Mykonos.* Athens: Melissa Publishing House, 1984.

Rossiter, Stuart. *Blue Guide Greece.* 4th ed. London: Ernest Benn Limited, 1981.

Rowse, Arthur E. "Among the Zagorochoria." *The Athenian* February 1990: 28-30.

Saïtas, Yanis. *Mani.* Athens: Melissa Publishing House, 1990.

Sakellariou, Becky Dennison. "The Caretta caretta: A Scramble to Life." *The Athenian* July 1982: 26-32.

Salamone, S. D. "Mount Athos: where heaven rests on earth's back." *The Athenian* August 1989: 24-29.

Salmon, Timothy. "The Vlachs: A Vanishing Race." *The Athenian* September 1982.

Sherrard, Philip. *The Pursuit of Greece.* Athens: Denise Harvey & Co., 1987.

Skapinker, Michael. "The Holy Mountain Experiences a Revival." *The Athenian* January 1984: 26-27.

Stamati, Helen-Fay. *Milies: A Village on*

Mount Pelion. Athens: The Athenian Press, 1989.

Stamatopoulou, Charoula. *Zagori.* Athens: Melissa Publishing House, 1988.

Stavroulakis, Nicholas. *Cookbook of the Jews of Greece.* Athens: Lycabettus Press, 1986.

Stoneman, Richard, ed. *A Literary Companion to Travel in Greece.* Harmondsworth, Middlesex, England: Penguin Books, 1984.

Tataki, A. B. *Sounion: The Temple of Poseidon.* Athens: Ekdotike Athenon S.A., 1985.

Tataki, A. B. *Corfu: History, Monuments, Museums.* Athens: Ekdotike Athenon S.A., 1985.

Thursby, J. M. "Shelter from the Storms." *The Athenian* April 1987: 40-41.

Tsigakou, Fani-Maria. *The Rediscovery of Greece: Travellers and Painters of the Romantic Era.* New Rochelle, New York: Caratzas Brothers, 1981.

Van Doren Stern, Philip. *Prehistoric Europe.* New York: W. W. Norton & Co., 1969.

Van Dyck, Karen, ed. *Greece.* Hong Kong: APA Productions (HK) Ltd, 1988.

Wagstaff, J. M. "A Small Coastal Town in Southern Greece: Its evolution and present condition." *The Town Planning Review* January 1967: 255-269.

Walker, Alan. "A Trip to the Southwest Peloponnisos." *The Athenian* June 1977.

Winnifrith, T. J. *The Vlachs: The History of a Balkan People.* London: Gerald Duckworth & Company Limited, 1987.

Winroth, Paul. *Working Watercraft of The Levant.* (unpublished ms.)

Woodhouse, C. M. *Modern Greece: A Short History.* London: Faber and Faber, 1968.

ACKNOWLEDGMENTS

PHOTOGRAPHER'S ACKNOWLEDGMENTS

I would like to thank the following for their help and support in the preparation of this book:
Ron Hall, whose advice proved invaluable. Hero Green, who gave me enough confidence to start speaking Greek. Tom Gazis of Athens, whose friendship and advice I value greatly. Manolis Lavdakis, his sons Fortis and Nicos and their families and also the Hourdakis family, who have given me such friendship and hospitality. Miltos Boukas of the Greek Tourist Board in Ioannina and the Society of Sarakatsanis in Ioannina. I would also like to thank all the people who agreed to be photographed for this book.

AUTHOR'S ACKNOWLEDGMENTS

Elizabeth Boleman-Herring would like to extend her thanks to Mr Gareth Walters, Mr Emil Moriannidis, the Canadian Archaeological Institute of Athens, Dr and Mrs Paris Raftopoulos, Mrs Patrick Leigh Fermor, and the many talented and dedicated contributors to *The Athenian: Greece's English Language Monthly.* Those interested in contacting the Sea Turtle Protection Society of Greece should write to one of those contributors, K Butterworth, at PO Box 51154, Kifissia, 145 10 Greece. She would also like to express her gratitude to the late Kevin Andrews, to Patrick Leigh Fermor, to Kimon Friar, and to Philip Sherrard, writers whose work has long served as an inspiration, and exhortation.

PUBLISHER'S ACKNOWLEDGMENTS

The publisher would like to thank Despina Katsirea and the London office of the National Tourist Organisation of Greece, and Gareth Walters for their help in producing this book.
The publisher would also like to thank the following for permission to reproduce quotations:
The Athenian, Greece's English Language Monthly, for S.D. Salamone's article.
The Benaki Museum, *Greece and the Sea,* A. Delivorrias and *Traditional Methods of Cultivations in Greece,* N. Psarraki-Belessioti and Aemilia Yeroulanou.
'In the Old Garden' by Yannis Ritsos, translation copyright © 1989 by N.C. Germanacos and 'Our Land' by Yannis Ritsos, translation copyright © 1989 by Andonis Decavalles; reprinted from *Yannis Ritsos: Selected Poems*

1938-1988 with the permission of BOA Editions Ltd, 92 Park Avenue, Brockport, NY 14420, USA.
Denise Harvey (Publisher) & Company, *The Pursuit of Greece,* ed. Philip Sherrard.
Greece on Foot, Marc Dubin © Reprinted with kind permission.
John Murray (Publishers) Ltd, *Roumeli: Travels in Northern Greece,* Patrick Leigh Fermor.
University of California Press, *Sappho: A New Translation,* Mary Barnard. Copyright © 1958 The Regents of the University of California; © renewed 1984 Mary Barnard.
Whilst every effort has been made to trace the copyright holders of all quotations included in this work, we apologize in advance for any unintentional omissions and would be pleased to insert the appropriate acknowledgment in any subsequent edition of this publication.